Language Generation and Evaluation Workshop 2011

(UCNLG+Eval 2011)

Held at EMNLP 2011

Edinburgh, Scotland, United Kingdom
31 July 2011

ISBN: 978-1-61839-245-9

Printed from e-media with permission by:

Curran Associates, Inc.
57 Morehouse Lane
Red Hook, NY 12571

CURRAN ASSOCIATES INC. proceedings.com

Some format issues inherent in the e-media version may also appear in this print version.

Printed by Curran Associates, Inc. (2011)

For permission requests, please contact the Association for Computational Linguistics at the address below.

Association for Computational Linguistics
209 N. Eighth Street
Stroudsburg, Pennsylvania 18360

Phone: 1-570-476-8006
Fax: 1-570-476-0860

acl@aclweb.org

Additional copies of this publication are available from:

Curran Associates, Inc.
57 Morehouse Lane
Red Hook, NY 12571 USA
Phone: 845-758-0400
Fax: 845-758-2634
Email: curran@proceedings.com
Web: www.proceedings.com

Introduction

The Workshop on Language Generation and Evaluation (UCNLG+EVAL) took place in Edinburgh on 31st July 2011, as part of EMNLP'11. It was the fourth of the UCNLG workshops which have the general aims

1. to provide a forum for reporting and discussing corpus-oriented methods for generating language;
2. to foster cross-fertilisation between NLG and other fields where language is automatically generated; and
3. to promote the sharing of data and methods for the purpose of system building and comparative evaluation in all language generation research.

Each of these workshops has had a special theme: at the first workshop (co-located with Corpus Linguistics 2005 in Birmingham, UK) it was the use of corpora in NLG; at the second (co-located with MT Summit 2007 in Copenhagen, Denmark) it was Language Generation and Machine Translation; at the third (co-located with ACL-IJCNLP 2009 in Singapore) it was Language Generation and Summarisation. The special theme of this fourth UCNLG workshop was Language Generation and Evaluation. The core aim was to showcase the latest developments in methods for evaluating computationally generated language across NLP, and to continue the discussion of future directions.

The call for papers issued at the end of January 2011 elicited a good number of high-quality submissions, each of which was peer-reviewed by three members of the programme committee. The interest in the workshop from leading NLG researchers and the quality of submissions was high, so we aimed to be as inclusive as possible within the practical constraints of the workshop. In the end we accepted four submissions as long papers and three as short papers.

The resulting workshop programme packed a lot of exciting content into one day. We were delighted to be able to include in the programme a keynote presentation by Prof Ehud Reiter, one of the most eminent researchers in NLG and a pioneer in task-based evaluation of NLG. Our technical programme was evenly divided between papers on new data resources for NLG (Galanis & Androutsopoulos; Viethen & Dale; Greenbacker et al.), and papers on generation methodologies (Curto et al.; Rajkumar & White; Copestake & Herbelot; de Kok). The programme also included a session of overview presentations of all eight past, current and in-preparation shared tasks in NLG. These overview presentations formed the basis for an interactive discussion session on the future of shared tasks in NLG.

We would like to thank all the people who have contributed to the organisation and delivery of this workshop: the authors who submitted such high quality papers; the programme committee for their prompt and effective reviewing; our keynote speaker, Ehud Reiter; the EMNLP 2011 Organising Committee, especially the workshops chair, Marie Candito; all the particpants in the workshop and future readers of these proceedings for your shared interest in this exciting area of research.

July 2011 Anja Belz, Roger Evans, Albert Gatt, and Kristina Striegnitz

Organizers:

Anja Belz, University of Brighton, UK
Roger Evans, University of Brighton, UK
Albert Gatt, University of Malta, Malta
Kristina Striegnitz, Union College, USA

Programme Committee:

Invited Speaker:

Ehud Reiter, Aberdeen, UK

Table of Contents

Conference Programme

Resources

09:05 *A New Sentence Compression Dataset and Its Use in an Abstractive Generate-and-Rank Sentence Compressor*
Dimitrios Galanis and Ion Androutsopoulos

09:35 *GRE3D7: A Corpus of Distinguishing Descriptions for Objects in Visual Scenes*
Jette Viethen and Robert Dale

10:05 *A Corpus of Human-written Summaries of Line Graphs*
Charles Greenbacker, Sandra Carberry and Kathleen McCoy

10:30 *COFFEE*

Shared Tasks Session

11:00 Stock taking: Task Summary presentations
12:30 Roadmapping: Interactive discussion on future of shared tasks

13:00 *LUNCH*

Invited Talk

14:00 *Task-Based Evaluation of NLG Systems: Control vs Real-World Context*
Ehud Reiter

Generation Methodologies

15:00 *Exploring linguistically-rich patterns for question generation*
Sérgio Curto, Ana Cristina Mendes and Luísa Coheur

15:20 *Linguistically Motivated Complementizer Choice in Surface Realization*
Rajakrishnan Rajkumar and Michael White

15:40 *COFFEE*

16:10 *Exciting and interesting: issues in the generation of binomials*
Ann Copestake and Aurélie Herbelot

16:40 *Discriminative features in reversible stochastic attribute-value grammars*
Daniël de Kok

A New Sentence Compression Dataset and Its Use in an Abstractive Generate-and-Rank Sentence Compressor

Dimitrios Galanis* and **Ion Androutsopoulos***+
*Department of Informatics, Athens University of Economics and Business, Greece
+Digital Curation Unit – IMIS, Research Center "Athena", Greece

Abstract

Sentence compression has attracted much interest in recent years, but most sentence compressors are extractive, i.e., they only delete words. There is a lack of appropriate datasets to train and evaluate abstractive sentence compressors, i.e., methods that apart from deleting words can also rephrase expressions. We present a new dataset that contains candidate extractive and abstractive compressions of source sentences. The candidate compressions are annotated with human judgements for grammaticality and meaning preservation. We discuss how the dataset was created, and how it can be used in generate-and-rank abstractive sentence compressors. We also report experimental results with a novel abstractive sentence compressor that uses the dataset.

1 Introduction

Sentence compression is the task of producing a shorter form of a grammatical source (input) sentence, so that the new form will still be grammatical and it will retain the most important information of the source (Jing, 2000). Sentence compression is useful in many applications, such as text summarization (Madnani et al., 2007) and subtitle generation (Corston-Oliver, 2001). Methods for sentence compression can be divided in two categories: *extractive* methods produce compressions by only removing words, whereas *abstractive* methods may additionally rephrase expressions of the source sentence. Extractive methods are generally simpler and have dominated the sentence compression literature (Jing, 2000; Knight and Marcu, 2002; McDonald, 2006; Cohn and Lapata, 2007; Clarke and Lapata, 2008; Cohn and Lapata, 2009; Nomoto, 2009; Galanis and Androutsopoulos, 2010; Yamangil and Shieber, 2010). Abstractive methods, however, can in principle produce shorter compressions that convey the same information as longer extractive ones. Furthermore, humans produce mostly abstractive compressions (Cohn and Lapata, 2008); hence, abstractive compressors may generate more natural outputs.

When evaluating extractive methods, it suffices to have a single human gold extractive compression per source sentence, because it has been shown that measuring the similarity (as F_1-measure of dependencies) between the dependency tree of the gold compression and that of a machine-generated compression correlates well with human judgements (Riezler et al., 2003; Clarke and Lapata, 2006a). With abstractive methods, however, there is a much wider range of acceptable abstractive compressions of each source sentence, to the extent that a single gold compression per source is insufficient. Indeed, to the best of our knowledge no measure to compare a machine-generated abstractive compression to a single human gold compression has been shown to correlate well with human judgements.

One might attempt to provide multiple human gold abstractive compressions per source sentence and employ measures from machine translation, for example BLEU (Papineni et al., 2002), to compare each machine-generated compression to all the corresponding gold ones. However, a large number of gold compressions would be necessary to capture all (or at least most) of the acceptable shorter rephrasings of the source sentences, and it is questionable if human judges could provide (or even think of) all the acceptable rephrasings. In machine translation, n-gram-based evaluation measures like BLEU have been criticized exactly because they cannot cope sufficiently well with paraphrases (Callison-Burch et al., 2006), which play a central role in abstractive sentence compression (Zhao et al., 2009a).[1]

Although it is difficult to construct datasets for end-to-end automatic evaluation of abstractive sentence compression methods, it is possible to construct datasets to evaluate the *ranking components* of generate-and-rank abstractive sentence compressors, i.e., compressors that first generate a large set of candidate abstractive (and possibly also extractive) compressions of the source and then rank them to select the best one. In previous work (Galanis and Androutsopoulos, 2010), we presented a generate-and-rank *extractive* sentence compressor, hereafter called GA-EXTR, which achieved state-of-the art results. We aim to construct a similar *abstractive* generate-and-rank sentence compressor. As part of this endeavour, we needed a dataset to automatically test (and train) several alternative ranking components. In this paper, we introduce a dataset of this kind, which we also make publicly available.[2]

The dataset consists of pairs of source sentences and candidate extractive or abstractive compressions. The candidate compressions were generated by first using GA-EXTR and then applying existing paraphrasing rules (Zhao et al., 2009b) to the best extractive compressions of GA-EXTR. Each pair (source and candidate compression) was then scored by a human judge for grammaticality and meaning preservation. We discuss how the dataset was constructed and how we established upper and lower performance boundaries for ranking components of compressors that may use it. We also present the current version of our abstractive sentence compressor, and we discuss how its ranking component was improved by performing experiments on the dataset.

Section 2 below summarizes prior work on abstractive sentence compression. Section 3 discusses the dataset we constructed. Section 4 describes our abstractive sentence compressor. Section 5 presents our experimental results, and Section 6 concludes.

2 Prior work on abstractive compression

The first *abstractive* compression method was proposed by Cohn and Lapata (2008). It learns a set of parse tree transduction rules from a training dataset of pairs, each pair consisting of a source sentence and a single human-authored gold abstractive compression. The set of transduction rules is then augmented by applying a pivoting approach to a parallel bilingual corpus; we discuss similar pivoting mechanisms below. To compress a new sentence, a chart-based decoder and a Structured Support Vector Machine (Tsochantaridis et al., 2005) are used to select the best abstractive compression among those licensed by the rules learnt.

The dataset that Cohn and Lapata (2008) used to learn transduction rules consists of 570 pairs of source sentences and abstractive compressions. The compressions were produced by humans who were allowed to use any transformation they wished. We used a sample of 50 pairs from that dataset to confirm that humans produce mostly abstractive compressions. Indeed, 42 (84%) of the compressions were abstractive, and only 7 (14%) were simply extractive.[3] We could not use that dataset, however, for automatic evaluation purposes, since it only provides a single human gold abstract compression per source, which is insufficient as already discussed.

More recently, Zhao et al. (2009a) presented a sentence paraphrasing method that can be configured for different tasks, including a form of sentence compression. For each source sentence, Zhao et al.'s method uses a decoder to produce the best possible paraphrase, much as in phrase-based statistical machine translation (Koehn, 2009), but with phrase tables corresponding to paraphrasing rules (e.g., "X

[1] Ways to extend n-gram measures to account for paraphrases have been proposed (Zhou et al., 2006; Kauchak and Barzilay, 2006; Padó et al., 2009), but they require accurate paraphrase recognizers (Androutsopoulos and Malakasiotis, 2010), which are not yet available; or they assume that the same paraphrase generation resources (Madnani and Dorr, 2010), for example paraphrasing rules, that some abstractive sentence compressors (including ours) use always produce acceptable paraphrases, which is not the case as discussed below.

[2] The new dataset and GA-EXTR are freely available from `http://nlp.cs.aueb.gr/software.html`.

[3] Cohn and Lapata's dataset is available from `http://staffwww.dcs.shef.ac.uk/people/T.Cohn/t3/#Corpus`. One pair (2%) of our sample had a 'compression' that was identical to the input.

is the author of Y" ≈ "X wrote Y") obtained from parallel and comparable corpora (Zhao et al., 2008). The decoder uses a log-linear objective function, the weights of which are estimated with a minimum error rate training approach (Och, 2003). The objective function combines a language model, a paraphrase model (combining the quality scores of the paraphrasing rules that turn the source into the candidate paraphrase), and a task-specific model; in the case of sentence compression, the latter model rewards shorter candidate paraphrases.

We note that Zhao et al.'s method (2009a) is intended to produce paraphrases, even when configured to prefer shorter paraphrases, i.e., the compressions are still intended to convey the same information as the source sentences. By contrast, most sentence compression methods (both extractive and abstractive, including ours) are expected to retain only the most important information of the source sentence, in order to achieve better compression rates. Hence, Zhao et al.'s sentence compression task is not the same as the task we are concerned with, and the compressions we aim for are significantly shorter.

3 The new dataset

To construct the new dataset, we used source sentences from the 570 pairs of Cohn and Lapata (Section 2). This way a human gold abstractive compression is also available for each source sentence, though we do not currently use the gold compressions in our experiments. We actually used only 346 of the 570 source sentences of Cohn and Lapata, reserving the remaining 224 for further experiments.[4]

To obtain candidate compressions, we first applied GA-EXTR to the 346 source sentences, and we then applied the paraphrasing rules of Zhao et al. (2009b) to the resulting extractive compressions; we provide more information about GA-EXTR and the paraphrasing rules below. We decided to apply paraphrasing rules to extractive compressions, because we noticed that most of the 42 human abstractive compressions of the 50 sample pairs from Cohn and Lapata's dataset that we initially considered (Section 2) could be produced from the corresponding source sentences by first deleting words and then using shorter paraphrases, as in the following example.

source: Constraints on recruiting are constraints on safety and have to be removed.

extractive: Constraints on recruiting have to be removed.

abstractive: Recruiting constraints must be removed.

3.1 Extractive candidate compressions

GA-EXTR, which we first applied to the dataset's source sentences, generates extractive candidate compressions by pruning branches of each source's dependency tree; a Maximum Entropy classifier is used to guide the pruning. Subsequently, GA-EXTR ranks the extractive candidates using a Support Vector Regression (SVR) model, which assigns a score $F(e_{ij}|s_i)$ to each candidate extractive compression e_{ij} of a source sentence s_i by examining features of s_i and e_{ij}; consult our previous work (Galanis and Androutsopoulos, 2010) for details.[5] For each source s_i, we kept the (at most) $k_{max} = 10$ extractive candidates e_{ij} with the highest $F(e_{ij}|s_i)$ scores.

3.2 Abstractive candidate compressions

We then applied Zhao et al.'s (2009b) paraphrasing rules to each one of the extractive compressions e_{ij}. The rules are of the form *left* ↔ *right*, with *left* and *right* being sequences of words and slots; the slots are part-of-speech tagged and they can be filled in with words of the corresponding categories. Examples of rules are shown below.

- get rid of NNS_1 ↔ remove NNS_1
- get into NNP_1 ↔ enter NNP_1
- NNP_1 was written by NNP_2 ↔ NNP_2 wrote NNP_1

Roughly speaking, the rules were extracted from a parallel English-Chinese corpus, based on the assumption that two English phrases ϕ_1 and ϕ_2 that are often aligned to the same Chinese phrase ξ are

[4] The 346 sources are from 19 randomly selected articles among the 30 that Cohn and Lapata drew source sentences from.

[5] We trained GA-EXTR on approximately 1,050 pairs of source sentences and gold human extractive compressions, obtained from Edinburgh's 'written' extractive dataset; see `http://jamesclarke.net/research/resources`. The source sentences of that dataset are from 82 documents. The 1,050 pairs that we used had source sentences from 52 out of the 82 documents. We did not use source sentences from the other 30 documents, because they were used by Cohn and Lapata (2008) to build their abstractive dataset (Section 2), from which we drew source sentences for our dataset.

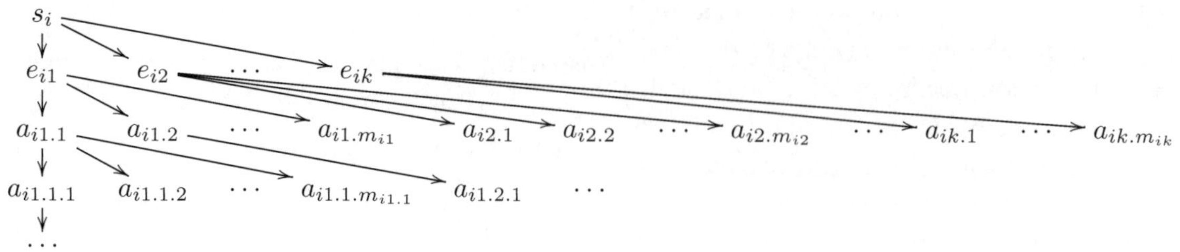

Figure 1: Generating candidate extractive (e_{ij}) and abstractive ($a_{ij...}$) compressions from a source sentence (s_i).

likely to be paraphrases and, hence, can be treated as a paraphrasing rule $\phi_1 \leftrightarrow \phi_2$. This *pivoting* was used, for example, by Bannard and Callison-Burch (2005), and it underlies several other paraphrase extraction methods (Riezler et al., 2007; Callison-Burch, 2008; Kok and Brockett, 2010). Zhao et al. (2009b) provide approximately one million rules, but we use only approximately half of them, because we use only rules that can shorten a sentence, and only in the direction that shortens the sentence.

From each extractive candidate e_{ij}, we produced abstractive candidates $a_{ij.1}, a_{ij.2}, \ldots, a_{ij.m_{ij}}$ (Figure 1) by applying a single (each time different) applicable paraphrasing rule to e_{ij}. From each of the resulting abstractive candidates $a_{ij.l}$, we produced further abstractive candidates $a_{ij.l.1}, a_{ij.l.2}, \ldots, a_{ij.l.m_{ij.l}}$ by applying again a single (each time different) rule. We repeated this process in a breadth-first manner, allowing up to at most $rule_{max} = 5$ rule applications to an extractive candidate e_{ij}, i.e., up to depth six in Figure 1, and up to a total of $abstr_{max} = 50$ abstractive candidates per e_{ij}. Zhao et al. (2009b) associate each paraphrasing rule with a score, intended to indicate its quality.[6] Whenever multiple paraphrasing rules could be applied, we applied the rule with the highest score first.

3.3 Human judgement annotations

For each one of the 346 sources s_i, we placed its extractive (at most $k_{max} = 10$) and abstractive (at most $abstr_{max} = 50$) candidate compressions into a single pool (extractive and abstractive together), and we selected from the pool the (at most) 10 candidate compressions c_{ij} with the highest language model scores, computed using a 3-gram language model.[7] For each c_{ij}, we formed a pair $\langle s_i, c_{ij} \rangle$, where s_i is a source sentence and c_{ij} a candidate (extractive or abstractive) compression. This led to 3,072 $\langle s_i, c_{ij} \rangle$ pairs. Each pair was given to a human judge, who scored it for grammaticality (how grammatical c_{ij} was) and meaning preservation (to what extent c_{ij} preserved the most important information of s_i). Both scores were provided on a 1–5 scale (1 for rubbish, 5 for perfect). The dataset that we use in the following sections and that we make publicly available comprises the 3,072 pairs and their grammaticality and meaning preservation scores.

We define the GM score of an $\langle s_i, c_{ij} \rangle$ pair to be the sum of its grammaticality and meaning preservation scores. Table 1 shows the distribution of GM scores in the 3,072 pairs. Low GM scores (2–5) are less frequent than higher scores (6–10), but this is not surprising given that we selected pairs whose c_{ij} had high language model scores, that we used the k_{max} extractive compressions of each s_i that GA-EXTR considered best, and that we assigned higher preference to applying paraphrasing rules with higher scores. We note, however, that applying a paraphrasing rule does not necessarily preserve neither grammaticality nor meaning, even if the rule has a high score. Szpektor et al. (2008) point out that, for example, a rule like "X acquire Y" $\leftrightarrow$ "X buy Y" may work well in many contexts, but not in "Children acquire language quickly". Similarly, "X charged Y with" $\leftrightarrow$ "X accused Y of" should not be applied to sentences about batteries. Many (but not all) inappropriate rule applications

[6]Each rule is actually associated with three scores. We use the 'Model 1' score; see Zhao et al. (2009b) for details.

[7]We used SRILM with modified Kneser-Ney smoothing (Stolcke, 2002). We trained the language model on approximately 4.5 million sentences from the TIPSTER corpus.

	Training part			Test part		
GM score	extractive candidates	abstractive candidates	total candidates	extractive candidates	abstractive candidates	total candidates
2	13 (1.3%)	10 (1.3%)	23 (1.3%)	19 (1.9%)	2 (0.4%)	21 (1.5%)
3	26 (2.7%)	28 (3.6%)	54 (3.1%)	10 (1.0%)	0 (0%)	10 (0.7%)
4	55 (5.8%)	29 (5.1%)	94 (5.5%)	51 (5.3%)	26 (6.2%)	77 (5.5%)
5	52 (5.5%)	65 (8.5%)	117 (6.9%)	77 (8.0%)	42 (10.0%)	119 (8.6%)
6	102 (10.9%)	74 (9.7%)	176 (10.3%)	125 (13.0%)	83 (19.8%)	208 (15.1%)
7	129 (13.8%)	128 (16.8%)	257 (15.1%)	151 (15.7%)	53 (12.6%)	204 (14.8%)
8	157 (16.8%)	175 (23.0%)	332 (19.5%)	138 (14.3%)	85 (20.3%)	223 (16.1%)
9	177 (18.9%)	132 (17.3%)	309 (18.2%)	183 (19.0%)	84 (20.1%)	267 (19.3%)
10	223 (23.8%)	110 (14.4%)	333 (19.6%)	205 (21.3%)	43 (10.2%)	248 (18.0%)
total	934 (55.1%)	761 (44.9%)	1,695 (100%)	959 (69.6%)	418 (30.4%)	1,377 (100%)

Table 1: Distribution of GM scores (grammaticality plus meaning preservation) in our dataset.

lead to low language model scores, which is partly why there are more extractive than abstractive candidate compressions in the dataset; another reason is that few or no paraphrasing rules apply to some of the extractive candidates.

We use 1,695 (from 188 source sentences) of the 3,072 pairs to train different versions of our abstractive compressor's ranking component, discussed below, and 1,377 pairs (from 158 sources) as a test set.

3.4 Inter-annotator agreement

Although we used a total of 16 judges (computer science graduate students), each one of the 3,072 pairs was scored by a single judge, because a preliminary study indicated reasonably high inter-annotator agreement.[8] More specifically, before the dataset was constructed, we created 161 $\langle s_i, c_{ij} \rangle$ pairs (from 22 source sentences) in the same way, and we gave them to 3 of the 16 judges. Each pair was scored by all three judges. The average (over pairs of judges) Pearson correlation of the grammaticality, meaning preservation, and GM scores, was 0.63, 0.60, and 0.69, respectively.[9] We conjecture that the higher correlation of GM scores, compared to grammaticality and meaning preservation, is due to the fact that when a candidate compression looks bad the judges sometimes do not agree if they should reduce the grammaticality or the meaning preservation score, but the difference does not show up in the GM score (the sum). Table 2 shows the average correlation of the GM scores of the three judges on the 161 pairs, and separately for pairs that involved extractive or abstractive candidate compressions. The judges agreed more on extractive candidates, since the paraphrasing stage that is involved in the abstractive candidates makes the task more subjective.[10]

	candidate compressions	average Pearson correlation
Extractive	112	0.71
Abstractive	49	0.64
All	161	0.69

Table 2: Inter-annotator agreement on GM scores.

3.5 Performance boundaries

When presented with two pairs $\langle s_i, c_{ij} \rangle$ and $\langle s_i, c_{ij'} \rangle$ with the same s_i and equally long c_{ij} and $c_{ij'}$, an ideal ranking component should prefer the pair with the highest GM score. More generally, to consider the possibly different lengths of c_{ij} and $c_{ij'}$, we first define the compression rate $\text{CR}(c_{ij}|s_i)$ of a candidate compression c_{ij} as follows, where $|\cdot|$ is length in characters; lower values of CR are better.

$$\text{CR}(c_{ij}|s_i) = \frac{|c_{ij}|}{|s_i|}$$

The GMC_γ score of a candidate compression, which also considers the compression rate by assigning it a

[8]The judges were fluent, but not native, English speakers.

[9]The Pearson correlation ranges in $[-1, +1]$ and measures the linear relationship of two variables. A correlation of $+1$ indicates perfect positive relationship, while -1 indicates perfect negative relationship; a correlation of 0 signals no relationship.

[10]The correlation that we measured on extractive candidates (0.71) is very close to the corresponding figure (0.746) that has been reported by Clarke and Lapata (2006b).

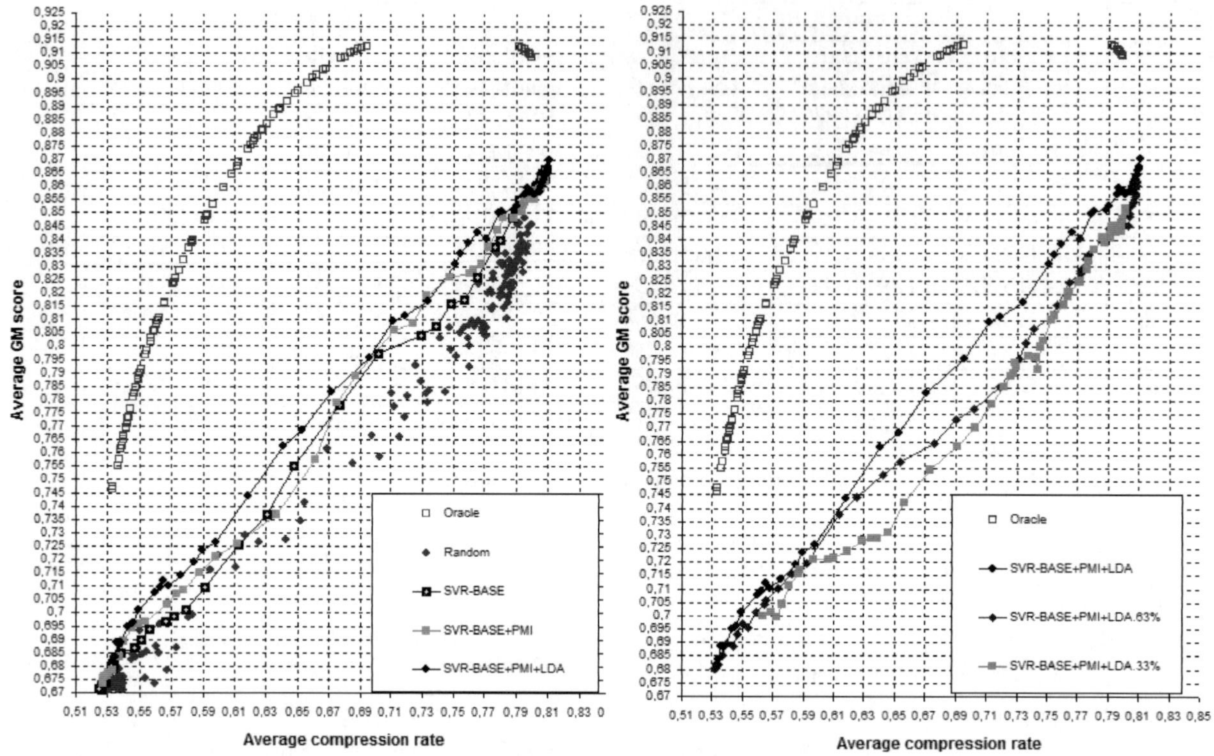

Figure 2: Results of three SVR-based ranking components on our dataset, along with performance boundaries obtained using an oracle and a random baseline. The right diagram shows how the performance of our best SVR-based ranking component is affected when using only 33% and 63% of the training examples.

weight γ, is then defined as follows.

$$\text{GMC}_\gamma(c_{ij}|s_i) = \text{GM}(c_{ij}|s_i) - \gamma \cdot \text{CR}(c_{ij}|s_i)$$

For a given γ, when presented with $\langle s_i, c_{ij}\rangle$ and $\langle s_i, c_{ij'}\rangle$, an ideal ranking component should prefer the pair with the highest GMC_γ score.

The upper curve of the left diagram of Figure 2 shows the performance of an ideal ranking component, an *oracle*, on the test part of the dataset. For every source s_i, the oracle selects the $\langle s_i, c_{ij}\rangle$ pair (among the at most 10 pairs of s_i) for which $\text{GMC}_\gamma(c_{ij}|s_i)$ is maximum; if two pairs have identical GMC_γ scores, it prefers the one with the lowest $\text{CR}(c_{ij}|s_i)$. The vertical axis shows the average $\text{GM}(c_{ij}|s_i)$ score of the selected pairs, for all the s_i sources, and the horizontal axis shows the average $\text{CR}(c_{ij}|s_i)$. Different points of the curve are obtained by using different γ values. As the selected candidates get shorter (lower compression rate), the average GM score decreases, as one would expect.[11]

The other curves of Figure 2 correspond to alternative ranking components that we tested, discussed below, which do not consult the judges' GM scores. For each s_i, these ranking components attempt to guess the GM scores of the $\langle s_i, c_{ij}\rangle$ pairs that are available for s_i, and they then rank the pairs by GMC_γ using the guessed GM scores. The lower points of the left diagram were obtained with a baseline ranking component that assigns a *random* GM score to each pair. The oracle and the baseline can be seen as establishing upper and lower performance boundaries of ranking components on our dataset.

4 Our abstractive compressor

Our abstractive sentence compressor operates in two stages. Given a source sentence s_i, extractive and

[11]The discontinuity in the oracle's curve for average compression rates above 0.7, i.e., when long compressions are only mildly penalized, is caused by the fact that many long candidate compressions have high and almost equal GM scores, but still very different compression rates; hence, a slight modification of γ leads the oracle to select candidates with the same GM scores, but very different compression rates.

abstractive candidate compressions are first generated as in Sections 3.1 and 3.2. In a second stage, a ranking component is used to select the best candidate. Below we discuss the three SVR-based ranking components that we experimented with.

4.1 Ranking candidates with an SVR

An SVR is very similar to a Support Vector Machine (Vapnik, 1998; Cristianini and Shawe-Taylor, 2000; Joachims, 2002), but it is trained on examples of the form $\langle x_l, y(x_l)\rangle$, where each $x_l \in \mathbb{R}^n$ is a vector of n features, and $y(x_l) \in \mathbb{R}$. The SVR learns a function $f : \mathbb{R}^n \rightarrow \mathbb{R}$ intended to return $f(x)$ values as close as possible to the correct $y(x)$ values.[12] In our case, each vector x_{ij} contains features providing information about an $\langle s_i, c_{ij}\rangle$ pair of a source sentence s_i and a candidate compression c_{ij}. For pairs that have been scored by human judges, the $f(x_{ij})$ returned by the SVR should ideally be $y(x_{ij}) = \text{GMC}_\gamma(c_{ij}|s_i)$; once trained, however, the SVR may be presented with x_{ij} vectors of unseen $\langle s_i, c_{ij}\rangle$ pairs.

For an unseen source s_i, our abstractive compressor first generates extractive and abstractive candidates c_{ij}, it then forms the vectors x_{ij} of all the pairs $\langle s_i, c_{ij}\rangle$, and it returns the c_{ij} for which the SVR's $f(x_{ij})$ is maximum. On a test set (like the test part of our dataset), if the $f(x_{ij})$ values the SVR returns are very close to the corresponding $y(x_{ij}) = \text{GMC}_\gamma(c_{ij}|s_i)$ scores, the ranking component will tend to select the same c_{ij} for each s_i as the oracle, i.e., it will achieve optimum performance.

4.2 Base form of our SVR ranking component

The simplest form of our SVR-based ranking component, called SVR-BASE, uses vectors x_{ij} that include the following features of $\langle s_i, c_{ij}\rangle$. Hereafter, if c_{ij} is an extractive candidate, then $e(c_{ij}) = c_{ij}$; otherwise $e(c_{ij})$ is the extractive candidate that c_{ij} was derived from by applying paraphrasing rules.[13]

- The language model score of s_i and c_{ij} (2 features), computed as in Section 3.3.
- The $F(e(c_{ij})|s_i)$ score that GA-EXTR returned.
- The compression rate $\text{CR}(e(c_{ij})|s_i)$.
- The number (possibly zero) of paraphrasing rules that were applied to $e(c_{ij})$ to produce c_{ij}.

4.3 Additional PMI-based features

For two words w_1, w_2, their PMI score is:

$$\text{PMI}(w_1, w_2) = \log \frac{P(w_1, w_2)}{P(w_1) \cdot P(w_2)}$$

where $P(w_1, w_2)$ is the probability of w_1, w_2 co-occurring; we require them to co-occur in the same sentence at a maximum distance of 10 tokens.[14] If w_1, w_2 are completely independent, then their PMI score is zero. If they always co-occur, their PMI score is maximum, equal to $-\log P(w_1) = -\log P(w_2)$.[15] We use PMI to assess if the words of a candidate compression co-occur as frequently as those of the source sentence; if not, this may indicate an inappropriate application of a paraphrasing rule (e.g., having replaced "charged Y with" by "X accused Y of" in a sentence about batteries).

More specifically, we define the $\text{PMI}(\sigma)$ score of a sentence σ to be the average $\text{PMI}(w_i, w_j)$ of every two content words w_i, w_j that co-occur in σ at a maximum distance of 10 tokens; below N is the number of such pairs.

$$\text{PMI}(\sigma) = \frac{1}{N} \cdot \sum_{i,j} \text{PMI}(w_i, w_j)$$

In our second SVR-based ranking component, SVR-PMI, we compute $\text{PMI}(s_i)$, $\text{PMI}(e)$, and $\text{PMI}(c_{ij})$, and we include them as three additional features; otherwise SVR-PMI is identical to SVR-BASE.

---

[12] We use LIBSVM (`http://www.csie.ntu.edu.tw/~cjlin/libsvm`) with an RBF kernel, which permits the SVR to learn non-linear functions. We also experimented with a ranking SVM, but the results were slightly inferior.

[13] All the feature values are normalized in [0, 1]; this also applies to the GMC_γ scores when they are used by the SVR. The $e(c_{ij})$ of each c_{ij} and the paraphrasing rules that were applied to $e(c_{ij})$ to produce c_{ij} are also included in the dataset.

[14] We used texts from TIPSTER and AQUAINT, a total of 953 million tokens, to estimate $\text{PMI}(w_1, w_2)$.

[15] A problem with PMI is that two frequent and completely dependent words receive lower scores than two other, less frequent completely dependent words (Manning and Schutze, 2000). Pecina (2005), however, found PMI to be the best collocation extraction measure; and Newman et al. (2010) found it to be the best measure of 'topical coherence' for sets of words.

4.4 Additional LDA-based features

Our third SVR-based ranking component includes features from a Latent Dirichlet Allocation (LDA) model (Blei et al., 2003). Roughly speaking, LDA models assume that each document d of $|d|$ words $w_1, \ldots, w_{|d|}$ is generated by iteratively (for $r = 1, \ldots, |d|$) selecting a topic t_r from a document-specific multinomial distribution $P(t|d)$ over K topics, and then (for each r) selecting a word w_r from a topic-specific multinomial distribution $P(w|t)$ over the vocabulary.[16] The probability, then, of encountering a word w in a document d is the following.

$$P(w|d) = \sum_t P(w|t) \cdot P(t|d) \tag{1}$$

An LDA model can be trained on a corpus to estimate the parameters of the distributions it involves; and given a trained model, there are methods to infer the topic distribution $P(t|\hat{d})$ of a new document $\hat{d}$.[17]

In our case, we treat each source sentence as a new document $\hat{d}$, and we use an LDA model trained on a generic corpus to infer the topic distribution $P(t|\hat{d})$ of the source sentence.[18] We assume that a good candidate compression should contain words with high $P(w|\hat{d})$, computed as in Equation 1 with $P(t|d) = P(t|\hat{d})$ and using the $P(w|t)$ that was learnt during training, because words with high $P(w|\hat{d})$ are more likely to express (high $P(w|t)$) prominent topics (high $P(t|\hat{d})$) of the source.

Consequently, we can assess how good a candidate compression is by computing the average $P(w|\hat{d})$ of its words; we actually compute the average $\log P(w|\hat{d})$. More specifically, for a given source s_i and another sentence σ, we define $\text{LDA}(\sigma|s_i)$ as follows ($\hat{d} = s_i$), where $w_1, \ldots, w_{|\sigma|}$ are now the words of σ, ignoring stop-words.

$$\text{LDA}(\sigma|s_i) = \frac{1}{|\sigma|} \cdot \sum_{r=1}^{|\sigma|} \log P(w_r|s_i)$$

[16]The document-specific parameters of the first multinomial distribution are drawn from a Dirichlet distribution.

[17]We use MALLET (`http://mallet.cs.umass.edu`), with Gibbs sampling (Griffiths and Steyvers, 2004). We set $K = 800$, having first experimented with $K = 200, 400, 600, 800, 1000$.

[18]We trained the LDA model on approximately 106,000 articles from the TIPSTER and AQUAINT corpora.

In our third SVR-based ranking component, SVR-PMI-LDA, the feature vector x_{ij} of each $\langle s_i, c_{ij} \rangle$ pair includes $\text{LDA}(c_{ij}|s_i)$, $\text{LDA}(e(c_{ij})|s_i)$, and $\text{LDA}(s_i|s_i)$ as additional features; otherwise, SVR-PMI-LDA is identical to SVR-PMI. The third feature allows the SVR to check how far $\text{LDA}(c_{ij}|s_i)$ and $\text{LDA}(e(c_{ij})|s_i)$ are from $\text{LDA}(s_i|s_i)$.

5 Experiments

To assess the performance of SVR-BASE, SVR-PMI, and SVR-PMI-LDA, we trained the three SVR-based ranking components on the training part of our dataset, and we evaluated them on the test part. We repeated the experiments for 81 different γ values to obtain average GM scores at different average compression rates (Section 3.5). The resulting curves of the three SVR-based ranking components are included in Figure 2 (left diagram). Overall, SVR-PMI-LDA performed better than SVR-PMI and SVR-BASE, since it achieved the best average GM scores throughout the range of average compression rates. In general, SVR-PMI also performed better than SVR-BASE, though the average GM score of SVR-BASE was sometimes higher. All three SVR-based ranking components performed better than the random baseline, but worse than the oracle; hence, there is scope for further improvements in the ranking components, which is also why we believe other researchers may wish to experiment with our dataset.

The oracle selected abstractive (as opposed to simply extractive) candidates for 20 (13%) to 30 (19%, depending on γ) of the 158 source sentences of the test part; the same applies to the SVR-based ranking components. Hence, good abstractive candidates (or at least better than the corresponding extractive ones) are present in the dataset. Humans, however, produce mostly abstractive compressions, as already discussed; the fact that the oracle (which uses human judgements) does not select abstractive candidates more frequently may be an indication that more or better abstractive candidates are needed. We plan to investigate alternative methods to produce more abstractive candidates. For example, one could translate each source to multiple pivot languages and back to the original language by using multiple commercial machine translation engines instead of, or in addition to applying paraphrasing

source	generated
Gillette was considered a leading financial analyst on the beverage industry - one who also had an expert palate for wine tasting.	Gillette was seen as a leading financial analyst on the beverage industry - one who also had an expert palate.
Nearly 200,000 lawsuits were brought by women who said they suffered injuries ranging from minor inflammation to infertility and in some cases, death.	Lawsuits were made by women who said they suffered injuries ranging from inflammation to infertility in some cases, death.
Marcello Mastroianni, the witty, affable and darkly handsome Italian actor who sprang on international consciousness in Federico Fellini's 1960 classic "La Dolce Vita," died Wednesday at his Paris home.	Marcello Mastroianni died Wednesday at his home.
A pioneer in laparoscopy, he held over 30 patents for medical instruments used in abdominal surgery such as tubal ligations.	He held over 30 patents for the medical tools used in abdominal surgery.
LOS ANGELES - James Arnold Doolittle, a Los Angeles dance impresario who brought names such as Joffrey and Baryshnikov to local dance stages and ensured that a high-profile "Nutcracker Suite" was presented here every Christmas, has died.	James Arnold Doolittle, a Los Angeles dance impresario is dead.
After working as a cashier for a British filmmaker in Rome, he joined an amateur theatrical group at the University of Rome, where he was taking some classes.	After working as a cashier for a British filmmaker in Rome, he joined an amateur group at the University of Rome, where he was using some classes.
He was a 1953 graduate of the Johns Hopkins Medical School and after completing his residency in gynecology and surgery, traveled to Denmark where he joined the staff of the National Cancer Center there.	He was a graduate of the Johns Hopkins Medical School and traveled to Denmark where he joined a member of the National Cancer Center there.
Mastroianni, a comic but also suave and romantic leading man in some 120 motion pictures, had suffered from pancreatic cancer.	Mastroianni, a leading man in some 120 motion pictures, had subjected to cancer.

Table 3: Examples of good (upper five) and bad (lower three) compressions generated by our abstractive compressor.

rules. An approach of this kind has been proposed for sentence paraphrasing (Zhao et al., 2010).

The right diagram of Figure 2 shows how the performance of SVR-PMI-LDA is affected when using 33% or 63% of the training $\langle s_i, c_i \rangle$ pairs. As more examples are used, the performance improves, suggesting that better results could be obtained by using more training data. Finally, Table 3 shows examples of good and bad compressions the abstractive compressor produced with SVR PMI LDA.

6 Conclusions and future work

We presented a new dataset that can be used to train and evaluate the ranking components of generate-and-rank abstractive sentence compressors. The dataset contains pairs of source sentences and candidate extractive or abstractive compressions. The candidate compressions were obtained by first applying a state-of-the-art extractive compressor to the source sentences, and then applying existing paraphrasing rules, obtained from parallel corpora. The dataset's pairs have been scored by human judges for grammaticality and meaning preservation. We discussed how performance boundaries for ranking components that use the dataset can be established by using an oracle and a random baseline, and by considering different compression rates. We also discussed the current version of an abstractive sentence compressor that we are developing, and how the dataset was used to train and evaluate three different SVR-based ranking components of the compressor with gradually more elaborate features sets. The feature set of the best ranking component that we tested includes language model scores, the confidence and compression rate of the underlying extractive compressor, the number of paraphrasing rules that have been applied, word co-occurrence features, as well as features based on an LDA model.

In future work, we plan to improve our abstractive sentence compressor, possibly by including more features in the ranking component. We also plan to investigate alternative ways to produce candidate compressions, such as sentence paraphrasing methods that exploit multiple commercial machine translation engines to translate the source sentences to multiple pivot languages and back to the original language (Zhao et al., 2010). Using methods of this kind, it may be possible to produce a second, alternative dataset with more and possibly better abstractive candidates. We also plan to make the final version of our abstractive compressor publicly available.

Acknowledgments

This work was partly carried out during INDIGO, an FP6 IST project funded by the European Union, with additional funding from the Greek General Secretariat of Research and Technology.[19]

References

I. Androutsopoulos and P. Malakasiotis. 2010. A survey of paraphrasing and textual entailment methods. *Journal of Artificial Intelligence Research*, 38:135–187.

C. Bannard and C. Callison-Burch. 2005. Paraphrasing with bilingual parallel corpora. In *Proceedings of ACL*, pages 597–604, Ann Arbor, MI.

D. Blei, A. Ng, and M. Jordan. 2003. Latent Dirichlet allocation. In *Journal of Machine Learning Research*.

C. Callison-Burch, M. Osborne, and P. Koehn. 2006. Re-evaluating the role of BLEU in machine translation research. In *Proceedings of EACL*, pages 249–256, Trento, Italy.

C. Callison-Burch. 2008. Syntactic constraints on paraphrases extracted from parallel corpora. In *Proceedings of EMNLP*, pages 196–205, Honolulu, HI.

J. Clarke and M. Lapata. 2006a. Constraint-based sentence compression: An integer programming approach. In *Proceedings of ACL-COLING*.

J. Clarke and M. Lapata. 2006b. Models for sentence compression: A comparison across domains, training requirements and evaluation measures. In *Proceedings of ACL-COLING*.

J. Clarke and M. Lapata. 2008. Global inference for sentence compression: An integer linear programming approach. *Journal of Artificial Intelligence Research*, 1(31):399–429.

T. Cohn and M. Lapata. 2007. Large margin synchronous generation and its application to sentence compression. In *Proceedings of EMNLP-CONLL*.

T. Cohn and M. Lapata. 2008. Sentence compression beyond word deletion. In *Proceedings of COLING*.

T. Cohn and M. Lapata. 2009. Sentence compression as tree to tree tranduction. *Journal of Artificial Intelligence Research*, 34:637–674.

S. Corston-Oliver. 2001. Text compaction for display on very small screens. In *Proceedings of the NAACL Workshop on Automatic Summarization*.

N. Cristianini and J. Shawe-Taylor. 2000. *An Introduction to Support Vector Machines and Other Kernel-based Learning Methods*. Cambridge University Press.

D. Galanis and I. Androutsopoulos. 2010. An extractive supervised two-stage method for sentence compression. In *Proceedings of HLT-NAACL*.

T. Griffiths and M. Steyvers. 2004. Finding scientific topics. In *Proceedings of the National Academy of Sciences*.

[19]Consult `http://www.ics.forth.gr/indigo/`.

H. Jing. 2000. Sentence reduction for automatic text summarization. In *Proceedings of ANLP*.

T. Joachims. 2002. *Learning to Classify Text Using Support Vector Machines: Methods, Theory, Algorithms*. Kluwer.

D. Kauchak and R. Barzilay. 2006. Paraphrasing for automatic evaluation. In *Proceedings of the HLT-NAACL*, pages 455–462, New York, NY.

K. Knight and D. Marcu. 2002. Summarization beyond sentence extraction: A probalistic approach to sentence compression. *Artificial Intelligence*, 139(1).

P. Koehn. 2009. *Statistical Machine Translation*. Cambridge University Press.

S. Kok and C. Brockett. 2010. Hitting the right paraphrases in good time. In *Proceedings of HLT-NAACL*, pages 145–153, Los Angeles, CA.

N. Madnani and B.J. Dorr. 2010. Generating phrasal and sentential paraphrases: A survey of data-driven methods. *Computational Linguistics*, 36(3):341–387.

N. Madnani, D. Zajic, B. Dorr, N. F. Ayan, and J. Lin. 2007. Multiple alternative sentence compressions for automatic text summarization. In *Proceedings of DUC*.

C.D. Manning and H. Schutze. 2000. *Foundations of Statistical Natural Language Processing*. MIT Press.

R. McDonald. 2006. Discriminative sentence compression with soft syntactic constraints. In *Proceedings of EACL*.

D. Newman, J.H. Lau, K. Grieser, and T. Baldwin. 2010. Automatic evaluation of topic coherence. In *Proceedings of HLT-NAACL*.

T. Nomoto. 2009. A comparison of model free versus model intensive approaches to sentence compression. In *Proceedings of EMNLP*.

J. F. Och. 2003. Minimum error rate training in statistical machine translation. In *Proceedings of ACL*.

S. Padó, M. Galley, D. Jurafsky, and C. D. Manning. 2009. Robust machine translation evaluation with entailment features. In *Proceedings of ACL-IJCNLP*, pages 297–305, Singapore.

K. Papineni, S. Roukos, T. Ward, and W. J. Zhu. 2002. BLEU: a method for automatic evaluation of machine translation. In *Proceedings of ACL*, pages 311–318, Philadelphia, PA.

P. Pecina. 2005. An extensive empirical study of collocation extraction methods. In *Proceedings of the Student Research Workshop of ACL*.

S. Riezler, T.H. King, R. Crouch, and A. Zaenen. 2003. Statistical sentence condensation using ambiguity packing and stochastic disambiguation methods for lexical-functional grammar. In *Proceedings of HLT-NAACL*.

S. Riezler, A. Vasserman, I. Tsochantaridis, V. Mittal, and Y. Liu. 2007. Statistical machine translation for query expansion in answer retrieval. In *Proceedings of ACL*, pages 464–471, Prague, Czech Republic.

A. Stolcke. 2002. SRILM - an extensible language modeling toolkit. In *Proceedings of the International Conference on Spoken Language Processing*, pages 901–904.

I. Szpektor, I. Dagan, R. Bar-Haim, and J. Goldberger. 2008. Contextual preferences. In *Proceedings of ACL-HLT*, pages 683–691, Columbus, OH.

I. Tsochantaridis, T. Hofmann, T. Joachims, and Y. Altun. 2005. Support vector machine learning for independent and structured output spaces. *Machine Learning Research*, 6:1453–1484.

V. Vapnik. 1998. *Statistical Learning Theory*. John Wiley.

E. Yamangil and S. M. Shieber. 2010. Bayesian synchronous tree-substitution grammar induction and its application to sentence compression. In *Proceedings of ACL*.

S. Zhao, C. Niu, M. Zhou, T. Liu, and S. Li. 2008. Combining multiple resources to improve SMT-based paraphrasing model. In *Proceedings of ACL-HLT*, pages 1021–1029, Columbus, OH.

S. Zhao, X. Lan, T. Liu, and S. Li. 2009a. Application-driven statistical paraphrase generation. In *Proceedings of ACL*.

S. Zhao, H. Wang, T. Liu, and S. Li. 2009b. Extracting paraphrase patterns from bilingual parallel corpora. *Natural Language Engineering*, 15(4):503–526.

S. Zhao, H. Wang, X. Lan, and T. Liu. 2010. Leveraging multiple MT engines for paraphrase generation. In *Proceedings of COLING*.

L. Zhou, C.-Y. Lin, and Eduard Hovy. 2006. Re-evaluating machine translation results with paraphrase support. In *Proceedings of EMNLP*, pages 77–84.

GRE3D7: A Corpus of Distinguishing Descriptions for Objects in Visual Scenes

Jette Viethen[1,2]
jette.viethen@mq.edu.au
[1]TiCC
University of Tilburg
Tilburg, The Netherlands

Robert Dale[2]
robert.dale@mq.edu.au
[2]Centre for Language Technology
Macquarie University
Sydney, Australia

Abstract

Recent years have seen a trend towards empirically motivated and more data-driven approaches in the field of referring expression generation (REG). Much of this work has focussed on initial reference to objects in visual scenes. While this scenario of use is one of the strongest contenders for real-world applications of referring expression generation, existing data sets still only embody very simple stimulus scenes. To move this research forward, we require data sets built around increasingly complex scenes, and we need much larger data sets to accommodate their higher dimensionality. To control the complexity, we also need to adopt a hypothesis-driven approach to scene design. In this paper, we describe GRE3D7, the largest corpus of human-produced distinguishing descriptions available to date, discuss the hypotheses that underlie its design, and offer a number of analyses of the 4480 descriptions it contains.

1 Introduction

Whenever we engage in any form of discourse we need to find a way to describe to our readers or listeners the entities that we are talking or writing about. This act of referring to real-world entities is one of the central tasks in human language production. Of course, it is also central when a machine is charged with the task of generating natural language, which makes referring expression generation (REG) an important subtask in any natural language generation (NLG) system.

It is therefore not surprising that REG has attracted a great deal of attention from the NLG community over the past three decades. A key factor that has led to the popularity of REG is the widespread agreement that the central task involved is *content selection*: choosing those attributes of a target referent that best distinguish it from other distractor entities around it (Dale and Reiter, 1995; van Deemter, 2000; Gardent, 2002; Krahmer et al., 2003; Horacek, 2003; van der Sluis, 2005; Kelleher and Kruijff, 2006; Gatt, 2007; Viethen and Dale, 2008).

Recent work in particular has concentrated on the development of algorithms concerned with the generation of context-free identifying descriptions of objects, as emphasised by three shared-task evaluation competitions (STECs) targeting this particular problem (Belz and Gatt, 2007; Gatt et al., 2008; Gatt et al., 2009). Referring expressions of this kind are often referred to as *distinguishing descriptions*. We are still far from a full understanding of how such descriptions should best be generated. Much work remains to be done before many issues, such as, for example, the generation of relational descriptions and over-specified descriptions or the number of the surrounding objects to be taken into account in visual settings, can be considered resolved.

Although many authors have explicitly or implicitly acknowledged the importance of generating referring expressions that sound natural (Dale, 1989; Dale and Reiter, 1995; Gardent et al., 2004; Horacek, 2004; van der Sluis and Krahmer, 2004; Kelleher and Kruijff, 2006; Gatt, 2007; Gatt et al., 2007), much of the original work in REG was neither developed based on empirical evidence about

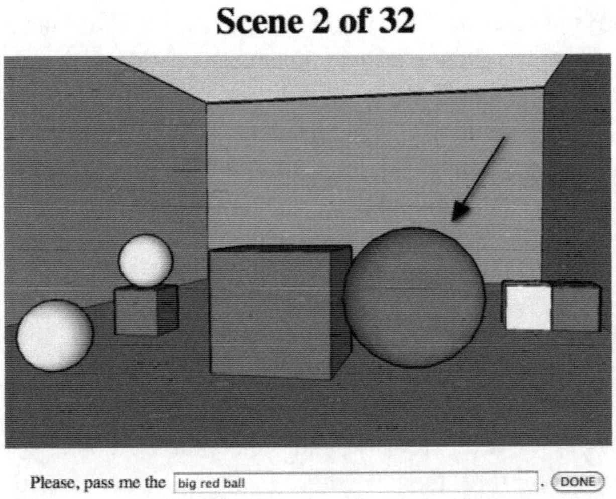

Figure 1: **The screen showing the first stimulus scene.**

how humans refer, nor evaluated against human-produced referring expressions. The REG STECs on the task of content determination form part of a recent trend towards more data-oriented development and evaluation of REG algorithms that responds directly to this concern (Gupta and Stent, 2005; Jordan and Walker, 2005; Gatt et al., 2007; Viethen et al., 2010; Belz and Gatt, 2007; Gatt et al., 2008; Gatt et al., 2009).

However, the existing data sets used in these experiments involve very simple and usually abstract visual displays of objects rather than coherent scenes. This is a reasonable starting point for bootstrapping research; but if we want to develop algorithms that can be used in real-world scenarios, we ultimately need to work with scenes which are much more realistic. At the same time, given the non-deterministic nature of choice in the production of natural language, corpora based on these scenes need to be very large, and should ideally contain referring expressions from as many different speakers as possible for each target referent in each referential scenario. The choice of stimuli and data collection procedure should provide a controlled environment that allows the isolation of a small number of factors influencing the choices that have to be made by the participants, in order to facilitate the replication of the same controlled environment for REG algorithms attempting the same reference task in an evaluation situation. The way forward, we believe, is to build a succession of corpora with incrementally more complex scenes.

In this paper, we describe the design of a data collection experiment for distinguishing descriptions and give an overview of the resulting corpus, which is, at 4480 instances, the largest corpus of distinguishing descriptions developed to date.[1] Consistent with the common focus on initial reference in visual scenes, we used visual stimuli containing a small number of simple objects (cubes and balls) in a 3D scene, similar to our much smaller GRE3D3 Corpus (Viethen and Dale, 2008), and elicited individual descriptions in the absence of a complicating preceding discourse. Additionally, we introduced factors that allow the study of the use of spatial relations in referring expressions by creating stimulus scenes that encourage the use of relations between objects, but do not require them. Most existing REG algorithms that can make use spatial relations between objects only do so if no distinguishing description can be found otherwise (Dale and Haddock, 1991; Gardent, 2002; Krahmer and Theune, 2002; van der Sluis and Krahmer, 2005; Kelleher and Kruijff, 2006), often based on the argument that mentioning two entities imposes a higher cognitive load than referring to only one entity. We are interested in investigating in how far this behaviour corresponds to the human use of spatial relations in distinguishing descriptions, as well as testing a number of concrete hypotheses about the factors that might lead people to use spatial relations.

2 Stimulus Design

The stimulus scenes used for the GRE3D7 corpus are three-dimensional scenes containing only simple geometric shapes, created in Google SketchUp. Each stimulus scene contains seven objects; these are grouped into three pairs of two and one single object. The target object is always part of one of the pairs and the second object of that pair is what we call the *landmark* object in these scenes. We attempted to place the target–landmark pair as close to the centre of the scene as possible to encourage the use of the target's direct object properties and its spatial relations to other objects, rather than its overall location in the scene, as in *in the left*. The other two object pairs were placed slightly further back to

[1] The corpus is available for download online at `www.clt.mq.edu.au/research/projects/gre3d7`.

the left and right of the target–landmark pair, and the single object was always placed in the far right or the far left of the scene. Objects were of one of two types (ball or cube) and otherwise distinguishable by their size and colour. Each object could be either large or small, and in each scene we used only two colours. Figure 1 shows a close-up of one of the scenes as presented to the subjects, and Figure 2 shows the complete set of stimulus scenes.

The design of the stimulus scenes was based on a number of hypotheses about the factors that might influence people's use of spatial relations to the landmark object. The two main hypotheses are concerned with the influence of the landmark object's size on its visual salience and the likelihood of the target–landmark relation being used in a referring expression:

Hypothesis 1: A large landmark is more salient than a small one because it occupies more of the visual space of a scene. Therefore, a large landmark is more likely to be mentioned in a referring expression via its spatial relation to the target referent than a small landmark.

Hypothesis 2: A landmark that shares its size with a number of other objects in the scene is less salient than one that is unique in size. Therefore, a landmark with unique size is more likely to be mentioned in a referring expression via its spatial relation to the target referent than a landmark with a common size.

Hypotheses 1 and 2 are concerned with the landmark's overall salience in the scene, or what is usually called *bottom-up* salience in the literature on visual attention (cf., Yantis, 1998). A second consideration that might influence the use of relations is the *top-down* salience of the target and landmark objects, as determined by the task the participants are performing. At the time when the landmark's visual salience is taken into account, the participants are focusing their attention on the target object. As the landmark is the closest object to the target, it is likely that the difference or similarity between these two objects plays a particularly important role in the decision whether to include the relation between them or not. Two conflicting hypotheses can be formulated here:

Hypothesis 3: The difference between the landmark and the target object impacts on the visual salience of the landmark because it impacts on the landmark's overall uniqueness in the scene. Therefore, a landmark that is visually different from the target is more likely to be included in a referring expression than one that looks similar to the target.

Hypothesis 4: The more similar the landmark and target objects are, the more they appear as one visual unit rather than two separate objects. If they are perceived and conceptualised as a visual unit, they are more likely to be mentioned together. Therefore, the more similar the landmark is to the target, the more likely it is to be included in a referring expression.

The fifth hypothesis that this experiment is designed to test concerns the preference that participants in psycholinguistic work have shown for vertical relations over horizontal ones (Lyons, 1977; Bryant et al., 1992; Gapp, 1995; Bryant et al., 2000; Landau, 2003; Arts, 2004; Tenbrink, 2004). To make sure that the landmark is never obscured by the target object, we use lateral relations rather than frontal ones in this experiment.

Hypothesis 5: A target placed on top of a landmark object is more likely to be described in terms of its spatial relation to the landmark than a target that is sitting directly adjacent to the left or right of the landmark.

We report the results of putting these five hypotheses to the test in Section 5.4. To be able to perform these tests systematically, the experiment was designed as a $2\times2\times2\times2\times2$ grid with the following five variables:

- LM_Size: the landmark is either large or small. [Large/Small]
- LM_Size_Rare: the size of the landmark is either a common size in the scene, or it is as rare as possible, and possibly unique. If it is common and the landmark is large, it shares its size with two of the objects; if it is small, with three. These numbers are not the same because in each scene in which the landmark

size was common, three objects were large and four small. In +LM_Size_Rare scenes that are also +TG_Size = LM_Size, the landmark shares size only with the target. Only if the scene is −TG_Size = LM_Size can the landmark's size be truly unique in the scene. [+/–]

- TG_Size = LM_Size: target and landmark are either the same size or different. [+/–]

- TG_Col = LM_Col: The target and the landmark are either of the same colour or different in colour. [+/–]

- Relation: The relation between the target and the landmark is either vertical (the target is on top of the landmark) or lateral, in which case the target is placed directly to the left or right of the landmark. [Vertical/Lateral]

This resulted in 32 experimental conditions. We created one stimulus scene for each of these conditions. We then split the stimuli into two trial sets along the factor TG_Size = LM_Size, so that this variable became a between-participant factor, while the other four are within-participant factors.

We followed a number of other criteria for the design of the stimulus scenes to ensure maximum experimental control over the factors influencing the content of the referring expressions provided by our participants:

Target uniqueness: The target was always distinguishable in terms of its inherent properties alone,[2] which means that the relation to the landmark or other external properties, such as the location in the scene, were never necessary to fully distinguish the target from all other objects in the scene.

Landmark uniqueness: As the target, the landmark was always distinguishable in terms of its inherent properties alone.

Colour balance: Each scene followed one of two colour schemes: either blue–green or red–yellow. The colour schemes were distributed in a balanced way across the five experimental variables, so that half of the scenes in each condition were blue–green and the other half red–yellow. The colour scheme was not expected to have an influence on the content of the referring expressions people produced. In each scene, four objects were of one colour of the colour scheme for this scene and three had the other colour.

Relation balance: The relation between the target and the object was never unique. One of the two other object pairs in each scene was arranged in the same spatial relation as the target–landmark pair and the third pair had the other relation. However, the objects in the pair with the same relation were never of the same types as the target and landmark, so that a description containing the type of the target, a relation to the landmark and the type of the landmark was always fully distinguishing.

Constant landmark and target types: The landmark was always a cube, in order to avoid scenes where the target would have to be balanced on top of a ball, which might look unnatural. The target was always a ball to make sure that the similarity in type between these two objects was always constant.

No obscured objects: The objects were placed in the scenes in such a way that no object occluded any other. In particular, as mentioned above, there were no frontal relations within the object pairs, to avoid larger objects obscuring smaller ones completely or to a large degree.

Figure 2 shows the 2×2×2×2×2 grid of the 32 stimuli scenes. Scenes 1–16, shown on a green background, constitute Trial Set 1, and Scenes 17–32, shown on a blue background, constitute Trial Set 2.

3 Procedure and Participants

The data gathering experiment was designed as a self-paced on-line language production study. Participants visited a website, where they first saw an introductory page with a set of simple instructions and a sample stimulus scene. Each participant was assigned one of the two trial sets containing 16 stimulus scenes each. After the instruction page, the scenes were presented consecutively in an order that was randomised for every participant. Below each scene, the participants had to complete the sentence

[2] We use the term *inherent property* to refer to any property of an entity which that entity has independent of the context in which it appears.

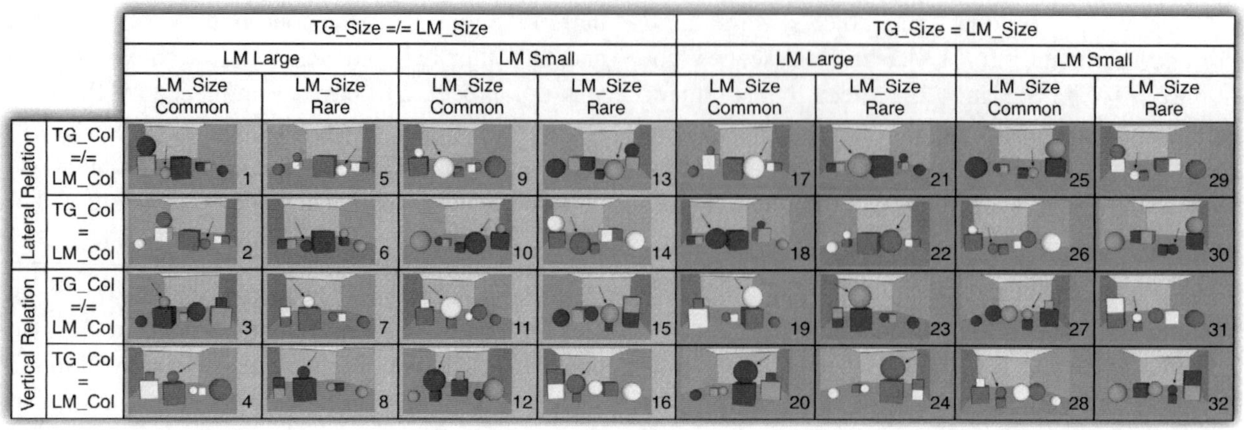

Figure 2: **The 32 stimulus scenes for GRE3D7**: The left half constitutes Trial Set 1 and the right half is Trial Set 2.

Please pick up the ... in a text box before clicking a button labelled 'DONE' to move on to the next scene, as shown in Figure 1. The task was to describe the target referent in the scene (marked by a grey arrow) in a way that would enable a friend looking at the same scene to pick it out from the other objects. To encourage the use of fully distinguishing descriptions, participants were told that they had only one chance at describing the object.

Before each of the 16 stimulus scenes, the participants were shown a filler scene, which means each participant had to describe 32 scenes in total. The main motivation for using filler scenes was to minimise the decline in relation use over time, which might otherwise happen if participants realised that relations were never necessary.

The filler scenes were also designed with the intention of making the experiment less monotonous, and to stop participants from noticing the strict design features of the stimulus scenes. In particular, each participant saw: four scenes with twelve objects in all four colours, as opposed to the two-colour schemes; two scenes containing only three objects; and ten further filler scenes which intentionally violated the above design criteria. The filler scenes for each participant were chosen such that in eleven or twelve scenes the target was a cube instead of a ball, in two scenes the landmark was a ball, in four scenes there was no obvious landmark close to the target, in eight scenes the target was unique (i.e. it could not be described by its inherent visual properties alone), in nine or ten scenes the target and landmark shared type, and in two or three scenes target and landmark were of the same size; for participants who saw Trial Set 2 all stimulus scenes also had a target and landmark of the same size.

The sequence of the 32 scenes that were shown to a particular participant was determined by the following three steps:

1. Pick the opposite trial set to the one that the last participant saw and randomise its order.
2. Pick the set of 16 filler scenes to be shown to this participant and randomise their order.
3. Interleave the two sets so that each stimulus scene is preceded by one filler scene.

After having described all 32 scenes in the trial, participants were asked to complete an exit questionnaire, which gave them the option of having their data discarded and asked for their opinion on whether the task became easier over time and any other comments they might wish to make.

The experiment was started by 318 native English speakers, of which 294 completed all 32 scenes. They were recruited by word of mouth via a widely-circulated call for participation and two electronic mailing lists.[3] The participants were predominantly in their twenties or thirties and mostly university-educated. A slight majority (54%) were female. None of them reported colour-blindness. Each referring expression in the corpus is tagged with an anonymous ID number linking it to some simple demographic data about the contributing participant, including gender, age, type of English spoken, and field of education.

[3]The Corpora List and the SIGGEN List.

4 Data Filtering and Annotation

Of the 294 participants who completed the experiment, five consistently used only type, although the target's type was never fully distinguishing in any of the stimulus scenes. For example, these participants described the target in Figure 1 simply as *ball*, which does not distinguish it from the two other balls in the scene. We discarded the data of these participants under the assumption that they had not understood the instruction that their descriptions were to uniquely identify the target. Two participants' data were discarded because they provided text that was unrelated to the displayed scenes. Of the remaining 287 participants, 140 saw Trial Set 2 and 147 saw Trial Set 1. The data from seven randomly-chosen participants from Trial Set 1 were discarded to balance the corpus in terms of the between-participant feature TG_Size = LM_Size. Each person described the 16 scenes contained in either of the trial sets, resulting in a corpus of 4480 descriptions in total, with 140 descriptions for each scene. No other corpus of referring expressions contains as many descriptions for each referential scenario from different speakers, which makes this corpus ideal for the study of speaker-specific preferences and non-deterministic choices in content selection.

Only five of the 4480 descriptions used the ternary spatial relation *between*, and one description mentioned two distinct spatial relations, one to the intended landmark and one to another object. The relation to the third object in these six descriptions was disregarded in the analysis presented here.

In order to be able to analyse the semantic content of the referring expressions, we semi-automatically annotated the inherent attributes and relations contained in each of them. The attributes annotated are

- type[ball, cube]
- colour[blue, green, red, yellow]
- size[large, small]
- location[right, left, front, top, bottom, centre]
- relation[horizontal, vertical]

Each attribute (except relation) is prefixed by either tg_ or lm_ to mark which of the objects it pertains to. For example, tg_size indicates that the size of the target was mentioned.

attribute	count	% of total 4480 descriptions	% of all 600 relational descriptions
tg_size	2587	57.8	–
tg_colour	4423	98.7	–
tg_location	81	1.8	–
relation	600	13.4	–
lm_size	327	7.3	54.5
lm_colour	521	11.6	86.8
lm_location	10	0.2	1.7

Table 1: **Attribute counts in GRE3D7**

In the 83 descriptions containing comparatives, such as Example (1), we ignored the second object that the target was being compared to. In all of these cases, the target's colour and type were also mentioned, which means that in the context of the simple scenes at stake here, Example (1) is semantically equivalent to Example (2).

(1) the smaller of the two red balls

(2) the small red ball

The question of how to deal with the relative nature of size is a separate, non-trivial, issue; see (van Deemter, 2000; van Deemter, 2006).

5 Analysis of the GRE3D7 Corpus

In this section we examine the content of the 4480 descriptions that make up the GRE3D7 Corpus. We first give an overview of the use of the non-relational attributes, and then proceed to investigate the hypotheses from Section 2 regarding the use of spatial relations.

The target object's type was mentioned in each description in the corpus, and each relational description contained the landmark object's type. Table 1 shows the number of descriptions containing each of the other attributes.

5.1 Sparing Use of location

Only 81 descriptions (1.8%) made reference to the target referent's location in the scene, as in Example (3); and of the 600 relational descriptions in the corpus, only ten (1.7%) contained the location of the landmark, as in Example (4).

(3) the large yellow ball on the left [Scene 9]

(4) the small ball next to the large cube on the left hand side [Scene 6]

There were no descriptions containing both tg_location and lm_location. This might indicate that participants who used a relation were more likely to conceptualise the target–landmark pair as a unit with just one location rather than as two individual entities. However, the corpus was not designed to investigate this issue and the numbers for use of location are too low to draw any definite conclusions.

5.2 Abundant Use of colour

Colour was used in the vast majority of descriptions: 98.7% of all descriptions included the colour of the target object and 86.8% of the relational descriptions included the colour of the landmark object. A high number of descriptions containing colour could be expected, as colour was part of the shortest possible minimal description not containing any spatial information (we call this the *inherent* MD of the target) for 20 of the 32 scenes (all but Scenes 17–24 and 29–32). However, the fact that colour was also included in the majority of the descriptions containing spatial information, in the form of a relation or the location, confirms previous findings to the effect that colour is often included in descriptions redundantly (Belke and Meyer, 2002; Arts, 2004; Gatt, 2007).

5.3 Utilitarian Use of size

The target's size was mentioned in 57.8% of all descriptions, and the landmark's size in 54.8% of the relational descriptions.

Considering that tg_size was part of the inherent MD in only 12 of 32 scenes (37.5%) of the stimulus scenes (Scenes 2, 4, 9–12, 18, 20 and 25–28), 57.8% seems like a high proportion of descriptions to be using this attribute. The use of tg_size for scenes where it was part of the inherent MD was at 90.2% very high, but this only accounts for just under 60% of all the descriptions that contained this attribute. The remaining 40% of descriptions containing tg_size were given for scenes in which this attribute was not strictly necessary to distinguish the target from the other objects.

Findings from eye-tracking experiments in psycholinguistics have shown that size is rarely used in situations where it adds no discriminatory power to the referring expression at all, and that it is more likely to be used to compare to or distinguish from other objects of the same type, while the same is not true for colour (Sedivy, 2003; Brown-Schmidt and Tanenhaus, 2006). Let us therefore consider in particular the scenes where tg_size was not part of the inherent MD, and look at the differing utility of tg_size in these scenes: 12 of the 20 scenes where tg_size was not necessarily part of the inherent MD (Scenes 1, 3, 5–8, 13–16, 17, 19, 21–24 and 29–32) nonetheless contained another object that shared the target's type (ball) but not its size (Scenes 1, 3, 17, 19, 21–24 and 29–32). In these scenes, tg_size remains a useful attribute to use, even if tg_type is also included.

Based on the psycholinguistic findings mentioned above, one might expect that the use of tg_size is higher for these scenes because here it helps distinguish from another object of the same type rather than only from objects of a different type. This hypothesis is supported by the data: tg_size was used in 45.6% of the descriptions for scenes where it was not part of the inherent MD but there was another object of same type and different size as the target. For scenes where tg_size could only distinguish the target from objects of the other type, it was only used in 27.3% of cases (χ^2=94.97, df=1, $p \ll .01$).

5.4 The Use of Spatial Relations

600 of the 4480 descriptions in the GRE3D7 Corpus (13.4%) mentioned a spatial relation. This was despite the fact that spatial information was not required in any of the stimulus scenes. Most existing approaches to spatial relations in REG would therefore never include a relation for any of the stimuli.

In this section, we examine the circumstances under which the participants of the GRE3D7 data collection experiment used the spatial relation between the target object and the intended landmark. We will first examine participant-dependent and temporal factors and then move on to analyse the impact that the design features of the scenes, described in Section 2, had on the use of relations.

General Factors

We first checked for broad participant-dependent preferences for or against using relations in the

GRE3D7 Corpus. The behaviour of participants who use an exclusive strategy of either always or never including a relation in their referring expressions would be easy to predict in a computational model and does not contribute to any variation across different scenes. In order to gain a clear understanding of this variation, we will concentrate on the data from participants who varied their use of relations between scenes.

Half of the participants (50.3%) adopted an exclusive strategy regarding the use of relations. However, the split between the two exclusive strategies was very uneven: 135 participants never used a spatial relation and only six used a spatial relation for all 16 stimulus scenes they saw. In the following, we analyse the data from the 139 participants who used a relation for some scenes but not for others. On average, these participants used a relation in 22.7% of their descriptions.

In (Viethen and Dale, 2008), we observed a 'laziness effect' whereby participants' use of relations decreased over the course of the experiment. A number of participants mentioned in the exit interview that they noticed over time that relations were never required and stopped using them. Such a conscious, or semi-conscious, adjustment masks people's natural propensity to use a relation in a reference situation where they come anew at the task rather than describing one object after another.

In the GRE3D7 collection experiment, each participant saw eight filler scenes in which spatial relations were required to distinguish the target. These filler scenes were included to stop participants from consciously noticing that relations were never required in the stimulus scenes. We hoped that this would reduce the laziness effect and thereby produce results that better approximate people's natural tendency to use a relation. However, Figure 3 shows that, despite the use of these filler scenes, the use of relations declined over the course of the experiment. Participants who did not follow an exclusive strategy clearly used more relations for scenes they saw early on than for those they saw towards the end. We divided the data set into quartiles in order to test the statistical significance of this decline. The falling trend was statistically significant at $p \ll .01$ (χ^2=55.42, df=3). However, any temporal effect in GRE3D7 should not interfere with

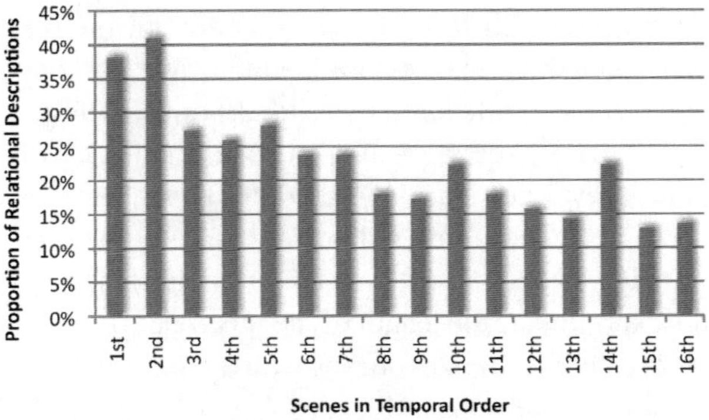

Figure 3: **Temporal effect on use of** relation

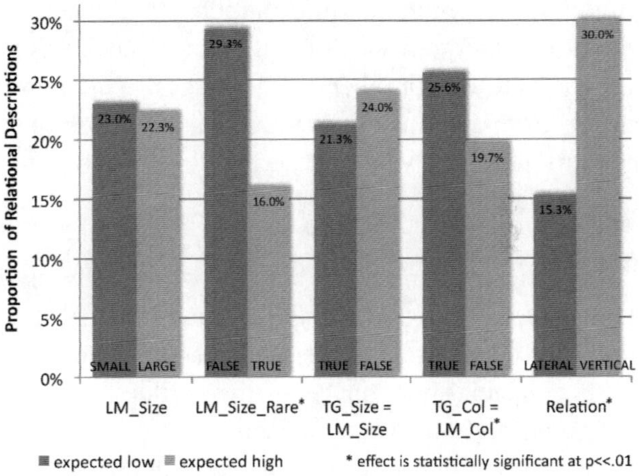

Figure 4: **Effect of design variables on use of** relation

between-stimulus effects, as the stimuli were presented in a randomised order.

Influence of Scene Features on Relation Use

We will now turn to the examination of **Hypotheses 1–5** from Section 2. Figure 4 shows the impact that each of the five variables of the scene design had on the use of relations. The left (green) columns represent the conditions for which we expected fewer relations to be used, and the right (yellow) columns represent the conditions for which we expected a higher use of relations, according to **Hypotheses 1–3** and **5**. **Hypothesis 4** expected the reverse results for TG_Size = LM_Size and TG_Col = LM_Col. All factors except LM_Size and TG_Size = LM_Size had a statistically significant effect.

Hypotheses 1 and **2**, which expected a large landmark with a rare or unique size to be more salient and therefore more likely to be used, are not supported by the data here. LM_Size did not have a reliable effect (χ^2=0.16, df=1, p>.6) and

LM_Size_Rare shows the opposite effect of the one we expected: a relation to a landmark with a common size is significantly more likely to be included in a referring expression than one to a landmark with a rare or unique size (χ^2=56.19, *df*=1, $p \ll .01$). On closer inspection, this is likely to be due to a factor that was not explicitly tested or controlled for in this experiment: the length of the inherent MD of the target referent. In most scenes with a common landmark size (all but Scenes 1, 3, 17, and 19), all three inherent attributes (size, colour and type) are necessary to distinguish the target from the other objects without using locational information. In all scenes where the landmark's size is rare or unique, colour and type suffice. In other words, targets which are harder to describe using inherent visual properties only are more likely to be described by a relation to a nearby landmark.

Hypotheses 3 and **4** predicted two mutually exclusive scenarios based on the assumption that the similarity between the target and the landmark object is of special importance, as the participant's visual attention is likely to be focussed on these two objects. **Hypothesis 3** predicted that a visual difference between the landmark and the target would increase the landmark's salience and therefore the use of the spatial relation to this landmark. **Hypothesis 4** predicted that high visual similarity between target and landmark might result in these two objects being conceptualised as a unit, which would increase the likelihood of both objects being mentioned. The target and landmark object were always of different types, so their similarity depends on their size and their colour, captured in the variables TG_Size = LM_Size and TG_Col = LM_Col. TG_Size = LM_Size did not show a significant effect on the use of relations (χ^2=2.29, *df*=1, $p > .1$). The effect of TG_Col = LM_Col favours **Hypothesis 4**, as a landmark of the same colour as the target is more likely to be included in the target's description than one that has a different colour from the target (χ^2=11.18, *df*=1, $p \ll 0.01$).

The variable Relation had the expected effect: A vertical relation is significantly more likely to be used than a lateral one (χ^2=69.00, *df*=1, $p \ll .01$). This confirms **Hypotheses 5**.

6 Conclusion

We have described the GRE3D7 Corpus, a collection of human-produced distinguishing descriptions that is considerably larger than any other existing corpus. The collection also uses scenes that are a degree more complex than those found in existing corpora; these are based on a principled design in order to provide a measure of control over what can be learned from the data. In this paper we have described the details of the collection experiment and have presented an analysis of the impacts that the design variables had on the content of the resulting descriptions. The main outcomes of this analysis are:

Colour is used in 99% of all descriptions. It is also used redundantly in 87% of all relational descriptions. This is in accordance with findings in other corpora and psycholinguistic studies.

Size is used when it is distinguishing. The size of the target referent was much more likely to be included when it was useful in distinguishing from another object in the scene, especially those of the same type.

Just over half of the participants follow an exclusive strategy for the use of relations. A large proportion of participants (135) opted to never use a relation, while a much smaller number of people (6) used a relation in all of their descriptions. The remaining 139 participants are responsible for the variation in the data, as they used a relation to describe the target in some but not all scenes.

The target–landmark relation is used more often if it is vertical than if it is lateral. This confirms previous psycholinguistic findings showing that humans prefer vertical relations and prepositions over horizontal, and in particular lateral, ones.

If a landmark shares colour with the target it is more likely to be used in a referring expression. This lends support to the hypothesis that visual similarity between target and landmark increases the likelihood of the relation between them being used.

The data thus sheds additional light on the nature of human-produced descriptions of objects in visual scenes. It also, of course, provides a rich corpus of data that can be readily used to evaluate the performance of computational algorithms for the generation of referring expressions.

References

Anja Arts. 2004. *Overspecification in Instructive Texts*. Ph.D. thesis, University of Tilburg, The Netherlands.

Eva Belke and Antje S. Meyer. 2002. Tracking the time course of multidimensional stimulus discrimination: Analysis of viewing patterns and processing time during same-different decisions. *European Journal of Cognitive Psychology*, 14(2):237–266.

Anja Belz and Albert Gatt. 2007. The Attribute Selection for GRE Challenge: Overview and evaluation results. In *Proceedings of the Workshop on Using Corpora for NLG: Language Generation and Machine Translation (UCNLG+MT)*, pages 75–83, Copenhagen, Denmark.

Sarah Brown-Schmidt and Michael K. Tanenhaus. 2006. Watching the eyes when talking about size: An investigation of message formulation and utterance planning. *Journal of Memory and Language*, 54:592–609.

David J. Bryant, Barbara Tversky, and Nancy Franklin. 1992. Internal and external spatial frameworks representing described scenes. *Journal of Memory and Language*, 31:74–98.

David J. Bryant, Barbara Tversky, and M. Lanca. 2000. Retrieving spatial relations from observation and memory. In Emile van der Zee and Urpo Nikanne, editors, *Cognitive interfaces: Constraints on linking cognitive information*, pages 94–115. Oxford University Press, Oxford, UK.

Robert Dale and Nicholas Haddock. 1991. Content determination in the generation of referring expressions. *Computational Intelligence*, 7(4):252–265.

Robert Dale and Ehud Reiter. 1995. Computational interpretations of the Gricean maxims in the generation of referring expressions. *Cognitive Science*, 19(2):233–263.

Robert Dale. 1989. Cooking up referring expressions. In *Proceedings of the 27th Annual Meeting of the Association for Computational Linguistics*, pages 68–75, Vancouver BC, Canada.

Klaus-Peter Gapp. 1995. Angle, distance, shape, and their relationship to projective relations. In *Proceedings of the 17th Annual Meeting of the Cognitive Science Society*, pages 112–117, Pittsburgh PA, USA.

Claire Gardent, Hélène Manuélian, Kristina Striegnitz, and Marilisa Amoia. 2004. Generating definite descriptions: Non incrementality, inference and data. In Thomas Pechmann and Christopher Habel, editors, *Multidisciplinary Approaches to Language Production*, pages 53–86. Walter de Gruyter, Berlin, Germany.

Claire Gardent. 2002. Generating minimal definite descriptions. In *Proceedings of the 40th Annual Meeting of the Association for Computational Linguistics*, pages 96–103, Philadelphia PA, USA.

Albert Gatt, Ielka van der Sluis, and Kees van Deemter. 2007. Evaluating algorithms for the generation of referring expressions using a balanced corpus. In *Proceedings of the 11th European Workshop on Natural Language Generation*, pages 49–56, Schloß Dagstuhl, Germany.

Albert Gatt, Anja Belz, and Eric Kow. 2008. The TUNA Challenge 2008: Overview and evaluation results. In *Proceedings of the 5th International Conference on Natural Language Generation*, pages 198–206, Salt Fork OH, USA.

Albert Gatt, Anja Belz, and Eric Kow. 2009. The TUNA-REG Challenge 2009: Overview and evaluation results. In *Proceedings of the 12th European Workshop on Natural Language Generation*, pages 174–182, Athens, Greece.

Albert Gatt. 2007. *Generating Coherent Reference to Multiple Entities*. Ph.D. thesis, University of Aberdeen, UK.

Surabhi Gupta and Amanda Stent. 2005. Automatic evaluation of referring expression generation using corpora. In *Proceedings of the Workshop on Using Corpora for Natural Language Generation*, pages 1–6, Brighton, UK.

Helmut Horacek. 2003. A best-first search algorithm for generating referring expressions. In *Proceedings of the 10th Conference of the European Chapter of the Association for Computational Linguistics*, pages 103–106, Budapest, Hungary.

Helmut Horacek. 2004. On referring to sets of objects naturally. In *Proceedings of the 3rd International Conference on Natural Language Generation*, pages 70–79, Brockenhurst, UK.

Pamela W. Jordan and Marilyn Walker. 2005. Learning content selection rules for generating object descriptions in dialogue. *Journal of Artificial Intelligence Research*, 24:157–194.

John Kelleher and Geert-Jan Kruijff. 2006. Incremental generation of spatial referring expressions in situated dialog. In *Proceedings of the 21st International Conference on Computational Linguistics and the 44th Annual Meeting of the Association for Computational Linguistics*, pages 1041–1048, Sydney, Australia.

Emiel Krahmer and Mariët Theune. 2002. Efficient context-sensitive generation of referring expressions. In Kees van Deemter and Rodger Kibble, editors, *Information Sharing: Reference and Presupposition in Language Generation and Interpretation*, pages 223–264. CSLI Publications, Stanford CA, USA.

Emiel Krahmer, Sebastiaan van Erk, and André Verleg. 2003. Graph-based generation of referring expressions. *Computational Lingustics*, 29(1):53–72.

Barbara Landau. 2003. Axes and direction in spatial language and spatial cognition. In Emilie van der Zee and Jon M. Slack, editors, *Representing Direction in Language and Space*, pages 18–38. Oxford University Press, Oxford, UK.

John Lyons. 1977. *Semantics*, volume 2. Cambridge University Press, Cambridge, UK.

Julie C. Sedivy. 2003. Pragmatic versus form-based accounts of referential contrast: Evidence for effects of informativity expectations. *Journal of Psycholinguistic Research*, 32(1):3–23.

Thora Tenbrink. 2004. Identifying objects on the basis of spatial contrast: An empirical study. In Christian Freksa, Markus Knauff, Bernd Krieg-Brckner, Bernhard Nebel, and Thomas Barkowsky, editors, *Spatial cognition IV: Reasoning, action, interaction*, number 3343 in Lecture Notes in Computer Science, pages 124–146. Springer, Berlin/Heidelberg, Germany.

Kees van Deemter. 2000. Generating vague descriptions. In *Proceedings of the 1st International Conference on Natural Language Generation*, pages 179–185, Mitzpe Ramon, Israel.

Kees van Deemter. 2006. Generating referring expressions that involve gradable properties. *Computational Linguistics*, 32(2):195–222.

Ielka van der Sluis and Emiel Krahmer. 2004. Evaluating multimodal NLG using production experiments. In *Proceedings of the 3rd International Conference on Language Resources and Evaluation*, Lisbon, Portugal, 26-28 May.

Ielka van der Sluis and Emiel Krahmer. 2005. Towards the generation of overspecified multimodal referring expressions. In *Proceedings of the Symposium on Dialogue Modelling and Generation at the 15th Annual Meeting of the Society for Text and Discourse*, Amsterdam, The Netherlands, 6-9 July.

Ielka van der Sluis. 2005. *Multimodal Reference, Studies in Automatic Generation of Multimodal Referring Expressions*. Ph.D. thesis, Tilburg University, The Netherlands.

Jette Viethen and Robert Dale. 2008. The use of spatial relations in referring expression generation. In *Proceedings of the 5th International Conference on Natural Language Generation*, pages 59–67, Salt Fork OH, USA.

Jette Viethen, Simon Zwarts, Robert Dale, and Markus Guhe. 2010. Dialogue reference in a visual domain. In *Proceedings of the 7th International Conference on Language Resources and Evaluation*, Valetta, Malta.

Steven Yantis. 1998. Control of visual attention. In Harold Pashler, editor, *Attention*, chapter 6, pages 223–256. Psychology Press, Hove, UK.

A Corpus of Human-written Summaries of Line Graphs

Charles F. Greenbacker, Sandra Carberry, and Kathleen F. McCoy
Department of Computer and Information Sciences
University of Delaware, Newark, Delaware, USA
[charlieg|carberry|mccoy]@cis.udel.edu

Abstract

We describe a corpus of human-written English language summaries of line graphs. This corpus is intended to help develop a system to automatically generate summaries capturing the most salient information conveyed by line graphs in popular media, as well as to evaluate the output of such a system.

1 Motivation

We are developing a system designed to automatically generate summaries of the high-level knowledge conveyed by line graphs found in multimodal documents from popular media sources (e.g., magazines, newspapers). Intended applications include making these graphics more accessible for people with visual impairments and indexing their informational content for digital libraries. Information graphics like line graphs are generally included in a multimodal document in order to make a point supporting the overall communicative intent of the document. Our goal is to produce summaries that convey the knowledge gleaned by humans when informally viewing the graphic, focusing on the "take-away" message rather than the raw data points.[1]

Studies have shown (Carberry et al., 2006) that the captions of information graphics in popular media often do not repeat the message conveyed by the graphic itself; such captions are thus not appropriate for use as a summary. Furthermore, while scientific graphs are designed for experts trained in their use for data visualization, information graphics in popular media are meant to be understood by all readers, including those with only a primary school education. Accordingly, summaries for these graphics should be tailored for the same general audience.

Research into information graphics by Wu et al. (2010) has identified a limited number of intended message categories conveyed by line graphs in popular media. Their efforts included the creation of a corpus[2] of line graphs marked with the overall intended message identified by human annotators.

However, we hypothesize that an effective summary should present the graph's intended message *plus* additional informational propositions that elaborate on this message. McCoy et al. (2001) observed that the intended message was consistently included in line graph summaries written by human subjects. Furthermore, participants in that study augmented the intended message with descriptions of salient visual features of the graphic (e.g., steepness of a trend line, volatility of data values). As part of the process of building a system to identify which visual features are salient and to describe them using natural language expressions, we collected a corpus of human-written summaries of line graphs.

2 Building the Corpus

We selected 23 different line graphs for use in building our corpus. This set covered the eight most-common intended message categories from the Wu corpus; only Point Correlation and Stable Trend were omitted. Table 1 shows the distribution of

[1] Users generally prefer *conceptual* image descriptions over *perceptual* descriptions (Jörgensen, 1998; Hollink et al., 2004).

[2] www.cis.udel.edu/~carberry/Graphs/viewallgraphs.php

Message Category	No. *(graphs)*
Big Fall (BF)	4 *(20–23)*
Big Jump (BJ)	2 *(18, 19)*
Changing Trend (CT)	4 *(8–11)*
Change Trend Return (CTR)	2 *(12, 13)*
Contrast Trend with Last Segment (CTLS)	2 *(14, 15)*
Contrast Segment with Changing Trend (CSCT)	2 *(16, 17)*
Rising Trend (RT)	4 *(1–4)*
Falling Trend (FT)	3 *(5–7)*
Total	**23** *(1–23)*

Table 1: Distribution of overall intended message categories in the set of line graphs used to build the corpus.

graphs across message categories.[3] Ten of the line graphs were real world examples in popular media taken from the Wu corpus (e.g., Figure 1). Another ten graphs were adapted from items in the Wu corpus – modified in order to isolate visual features so that their individual effects could be analyzed (e.g., Figure 2). The remaining three line graphs were created specifically to fill a gap in the coverage of intended messages and visual features for which no good example was available (e.g., Figure 3). Our goal was to include as many different combinations of message category and visual features as possible (e.g., for graphs containing a dramatic change in values because of a big jump or fall, we included examples which sustained the change as well as others that did not sustain the change).

69 subjects participated in our study. All were native English speakers, 18 years of age or older, without major sight impairments, and enrolled in an introductory computer science course at a university in the US. They received a small amount of extra credit in their course for participating in this study.

Each participant was given the full set of 23 line graphs in differing orders. With each graph, the subjects were presented with an initial summary sentence describing the overall intended message of the graphic, as identified by a human annotator. The captions for Figures 1, 2, and 3 each contain the corresponding initial summary sentence that was provided to the participants. Participants were tasked with writing additional sentences so that the completed summary of each line graph captured the most important information conveyed by the graphic, finishing as many or as few of the 23 graphs as they wished during a single one-hour session.

[3]Category descriptions can be found in (Wu et al., 2010).

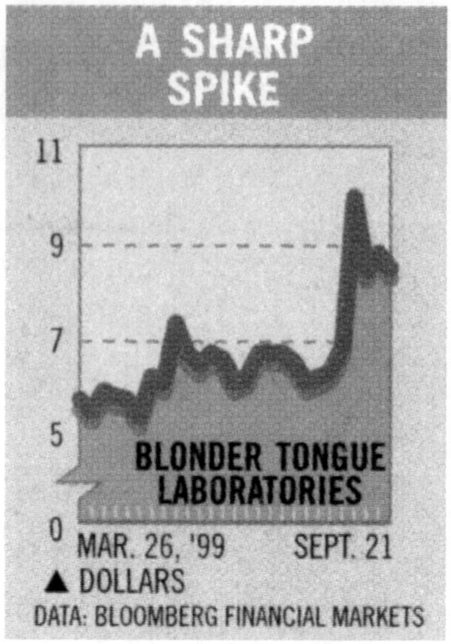

Figure 1: From "This Cable Outfit Is Getting Tuned In" in *Businessweek* magazine, Oct 4, 1999. (Initial sentence: "*This line graph shows a big jump in Blonder Tongue Laboratories stock price in August '99.*")

Participants were told that we were developing a system to convey an initial summary of an information graphic from popular media (as opposed to textbooks or scientific articles) to blind users via speech. We indicated that the summaries they write should be brief (though we did not specify any length requirements), but ought to include all essential information provided by the graphic. Subjects were only given the graphics and did not receive the original article text (if any existed) that accompanied the real-world graphs. Finally, the participants were told that a person able to see the graphics should not think that the summaries they wrote were misleading.

3 Corpus Characteristics

A total of 965 summaries were collected, ranging from 37 to 49 summaries for each individual line graph. Table 2 offers some descriptive statistics for the corpus as a whole, while Table 3 lists the ten most commonly-occurring content words.

Sample summary 1 (*18-4.txt*) was written for Figure 1, summary 2 (*7-40.txt*) for Figure 2, and summaries 3 (*9-2.txt*) and 4 (*9-5.txt*) both for Figure 3:

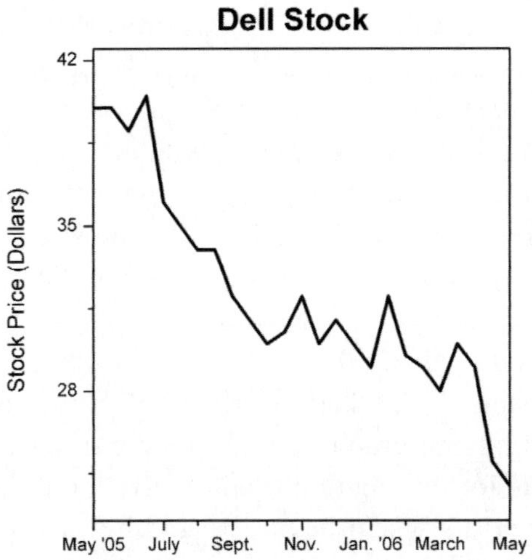

Figure 2: Adapted from original in "Dell goes with a few AMD chips," *USA Today*, Oct 19, 2006. (Initial sentence: "*This line graph shows a falling trend in Dell stock from May '05 to May '06.*")

From March 26, 1999 the graph rises and declines up until August 1999 where it rises at about a 90-degree angle then declines again. (1)

The graph peaked in July '05 but then sharply decreased after that. It had several sharp inclines and declines and ended with a shaper decline from March '06 to May '06. (2)

February has a much larger amount of jackets sold than the other months shown. From december to january, there was a slight drop in the amount of jackets sold and then a large spike from january to february. (3)

The values in November and May are pretty close, with both being around 37 or 38 jackets. At its peak (February), around 47 jackets were sold. (4)

4 Potential Usage

To our knowledge, this is the first and only publicly-available corpus of line graph summaries. It has several possible applications in both natural language generation and evaluation tasks. By finding and examining patterns in the summaries, we can discover which propositions are found to be most salient for certain kinds of graphs. We are currently analyzing the collected corpus for this very purpose – to identify relationships between visual features, intended messages, and the relative importance of including corresponding propositions in a summary (e.g., *volatility* is more salient in Figure 2 than Figure 3).

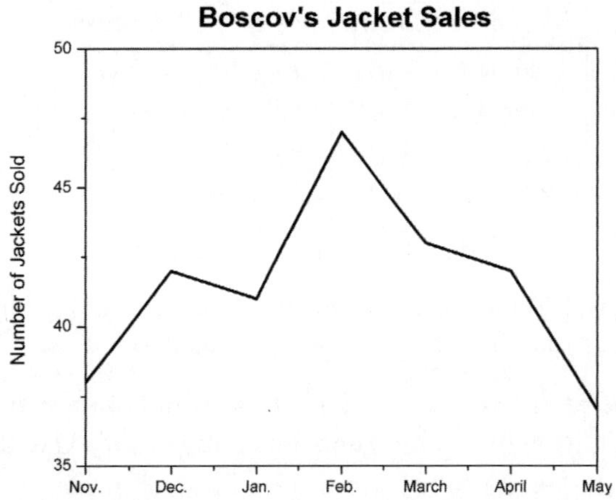

Figure 3: Sample line graph created for this study. (Initial sentence: "*This line graph shows a rising trend in Boscov's jacket sales from November to February followed by a falling trend through May.*")

Metric	Value
total characters	213,261
total words (w)	45,217
total sentences	2,184
characters per word	4.72
words per sentence	20.70
sentences per summary	2.26
unique words (u)	1,831
lexical diversity (w/u)	24.70
hapax legomena	699
pct. of unique words	38.18%
pct. of total words	1.55%

Table 2: Various descriptive statistics for the corpus.

Not only does this corpus offer insight into what humans perceive to be the most important information conveyed by line graphs, it provides a large set of real-world expressions from which to draw when crafting the surface realization forms for summaries of line graphs. From a generation perspective, this collection of summaries offers copious examples of the expressions human use to describe characteristics of information graphics. The corpus could also be used to determine the proper structural characteristics of a line graph summary (e.g., when multiple information is included, how propositions are aggregated into sentences, which details come first).

The evaluation of graph understanding systems will also benefit from the use of this corpus. It will enable comparisons between system and human-

Word	Count	Word	Count
graph	715	*stock*	287
price	349	*increase*	280
august	305	*may*	279
dollars	300	*decrease*	192
around	299	*trend*	183

Table 3: The ten most frequently occurring words in the corpus (omitting stopwords and punctuation).

generated descriptions at the propositional (content) level, as well as judgments involving clarity and coherence. The set of summaries for each graph may be used as a "gold standard" against which to compare automatically-generated summaries in preference judgment experiments involving human judges.

We are currently developing rules for identifying the most salient information conveyed by a given line graph based on an analysis of this corpus, and will also use the expressions in the collected summaries as examples for surface realization during the summary generation process. Additionally, we are planning to use the corpus during part of the evaluation phase of our project, by asking human judges to compare these human-written summaries against our system's output across multiple dimensions of preference. It may also be useful to perform some additional human subjects experiments to determine which summaries in the corpus are found to be most helpful and understandable.

5 Related Work

Prior to this study, we performed an initial investigation based on a questionnaire similar to the one used by Demir (2010) for bar charts. A group of human subjects was asked to review several line graphs and indicate how important it would be to include various propositions in an initial summary of each graphic. Although this method was effective with bar charts, it proved to be far too cumbersome to work with line graphs. Bar charts are somewhat simpler, propositionally-speaking, as there are fewer informational propositions that can be extracted from data represented as discrete bars rather than as a continuous data series in a line graph. It required far more effort for subjects to evaluate the relative importance of each individual proposition than to simply provide (in the form of a written summary) the set of propositions they considered to be most important. In the end, the summary-based approach allowed for a more direct examination of salience judgments without subjects being constrained or influenced by the questions and structure of the questionnaire-based approach, with the added bonus of producing a reusable corpus of human-written summaries of line graphs.

McCoy et al. (2001) performed a study in which participants were asked to write brief summaries for a series of line graphs. While they did not release a corpus for distribution, their analysis did suggest that a graph's visual features could be used to help select salient propositions to include in a summary.

Although several corpora exist for general image descriptions, we are unaware of any other corpora of human-written summaries for information graphics. Jörgensen (1998) collected unconstrained descriptions of pictorial images, while Hollink et al. (2004) analyzed descriptions of mental images formed by subjects to illustrate a given text passage. Aker and Gaizauskas (2010) built a corpus of human-generated captions for location-related images. Large collections of general image captions have been assembled for information retrieval tasks (Smeaton and Quigley, 1996; Tribble, 2010). Roy (2002) evaluated automatically-generated descriptions of visual scenes against human-generated descriptions. The developers of the iGraph-Lite system (Ferres et al., 2007) released a corpus of descriptions for over 500 graphs collected from Statistics Canada, but these descriptions were generated automatically by their system and not written by human authors. Additionally, the descriptions contained in their corpus focus on the quantitative data presented in the graphics rather than the high-level message, and tend to vary only slightly between graphs.[4]

Since using corpus texts as a "gold standard" in generation and evaluation can be tricky (Reiter and Sripada, 2002), we tried to mitigate some of the common problems, including giving participants as much time as they wanted for each summary to avoid "hurried writing." However, as we intend to use this corpus to understand which propositions humans find salient for line graphs, as well as generat-

[4]The iGraph-Lite system provides the same information for each instance of a graph type (i.e., all summaries of line graphs contain the same sorts of information).

ing and evaluating new summaries, a larger collection of examples written by many authors for several different graphics was more desirable than a smaller corpus of higher-quality texts from fewer authors.

6 Availability

The corpus is freely available for download[5] without restrictions under an open source license.

The structure of the corpus is as follows. The "summaries" directory consists of a series of subdirectories numbered 1-23 containing the summaries for all 23 line graphs, with each summary stored in a separate file (encoded as ASCII text). The files are named according to the graph they are associated with and their position in that graph's collection (e.g., *8-10.txt* is the 10th summary for the 8th line graph, and is located in the directory named *8*).

The root of the distribution package contains a directory of original image files for the line graphs (named "line graphs"), the initial sentences describing each graph's intended message (which was provided to the participants) in sentences.txt, and a README file describing the corpus layout.

The corpus is easily loaded with NLTK (Loper and Bird, 2002) using these Python commands:

```
from nltk.corpus import PlaintextCorpusReader
LGSroot = './LGSummaryCorpus/summaries'
corpus = PlaintextCorpusReader(LGSroot, '.*')
```

Acknowledgments

This work was supported in part by the National Institute on Disability and Rehabilitation Research under Grant No. H133G080047.

References

Ahmet Aker and Robert Gaizauskas. 2010. Model summaries for location-related images. In *Proceedings of the Seventh Conference on International Language Resources and Evaluation*, LREC '10, pages 3119–3124, Malta, May. ELRA.

Sandra Carberry, Stephanie Elzer, and Seniz Demir. 2006. Information graphics: an untapped resource for digital libraries. In *Proceedings of the 29th Annual International ACM SIGIR Conference on Research and Development in Information Retrieval*, SIGIR '06, pages 581–588, Seattle, August. ACM.

Seniz Demir. 2010. *SIGHT for Visually Impaired Users: Summarizing Information Graphics Textually*. Ph.D. thesis, University of Delaware, February.

Leo Ferres, Petro Verkhogliad, Gitte Lindgaard, Louis Boucher, Antoine Chretien, and Martin Lachance. 2007. Improving accessibility to statistical graphs: the iGraph-Lite system. In *Proceedings of the 9th International ACM SIGACCESS Conference on Computers and Accessibility*, ASSETS '07, pages 67–74, Tempe, October. ACM.

L. Hollink, A. Th. Schreiber, B. J. Wielinga, and M. Worring. 2004. Classification of user image descriptions. *International Journal of Human-Computer Studies*, 61(5):601–626, November.

Corinne Jörgensen. 1998. Attributes of images in describing tasks. *Information Processing and Management*, 34:161–174, March–May.

Edward Loper and Steven Bird. 2002. NLTK: The natural language toolkit. In *Proceedings of the ACL-02 Workshop on Effective Tools and Methodologies for Teaching Natural Language Processing and Computational Linguistics*, pages 63–70, Philadelphia, July. ACL.

Kathleen F. McCoy, M. Sandra Carberry, Tom Roper, and Nancy Green. 2001. Towards generating textual summaries of graphs. In *Proceedings of the 1st International Conference on Universal Access in Human-Computer Interaction*, UAHCI 2001, pages 695–699, New Orleans, August. Lawrence Erlbaum.

Ehud Reiter and Somayajulu Sripada. 2002. Should corpora texts be gold standards for NLG? In *Proceedings of the Second International Conference on Natural Language Generation*, INLG 2002, pages 97–104, Harriman, New York, July. ACL.

Deb K. Roy. 2002. Learning visually grounded words and syntax for a scene description task. *Computer Speech & Language*, 16(3–4):353–385, July–October.

Alan F. Smeaton and Ian Quigley. 1996. Experiments on using semantic distances between words in image caption retrieval. In *Proceedings of the 19th Annual International ACM SIGIR Conference on Research and Development in Information Retrieval*, SIGIR '96, pages 174–180, Zurich, August. ACM.

Alicia Tribble. 2010. *Textual Inference for Retrieving Labeled Object Descriptions*. Ph.D. thesis, Carnegie Mellon University, April.

Peng Wu, Sandra Carberry, Stephanie Elzer, and Daniel Chester. 2010. Recognizing the intended message of line graphs. In *Proceedings of the Sixth International Conference on the Theory and Application of Diagrams*, Diagrams 2010, pages 220–234, Portland, Oregon, August. Springer-Verlag.

[5] www.cis.udel.edu/~mccoy/corpora

Task-Based Evaluation of NLG Systems: Control vs Real-World Context

Ehud Reiter
Dept of Computing Science
University of Aberdeen
e.reiter@abdn.ac.uk

Abstract

Currently there is little agreement about, or even discussion of, methodologies for task-based evaluation of NLG systems. I discuss one specific issue in this area, namely the importance of control vs the importance of ecological validity (real-world context), and suggest that perhaps we need to put more emphasis on ecological validity in NLG evaluations.

1 Introduction

Task-based extrinsic evaluation of a Natural Language Generation (NLG) system involves measuring the impact of an NLG system on how well subjects perform a task. It is usually regarded as the 'gold standard' for NLG evaluation, and it is the only type of evaluation which will be seriously considered by many external user communities.

Despite the importance of task-based evaluations, however, there is surprisingly little discussion (or agreement) in the NLG community about how these should be carried out. In recent years there has been a fair amount of discussion about the appropriate use of corpus-based metrics, and there seems (de facto) to be some level of agreement about evaluations based on opinions of human subjects. But there is little discussion and much diversity in task-based evaluation methodology.

In this paper I focus on one one specific methodological issue, which is the relative importance of control and ecological validity (real-world context). An ideal task-based evaluation would be controlled, that is the impact of NLG texts would be compared against the impact of controlled or baseline texts in a manner which minimises confounding factors. It would also be ecologically valid, that is the evaluation would be carried out by representative real-world users in a real-world context while performing real-world tasks. Unfortunately, because of pragmatic constraints including time, money, and ethical approval, it is not always possible to achieve both of these goals. So which is more important?

The methodologies currently used for task-based evaluation in NLG largely derive from the Human-Computer Interaction community, which in turn are largely based on methodologies for experiments in cognitive psychology. Now, psychologists place much more emphasis on control than on ecological validity; they regard control as absolutely essential, but (with some exceptions) they see little wrong with conducting experiments on unrepresentative subjects (undergraduates) in artificial contexts (psychology labs). Indeed many psychologists are now embracing web-based experiments, where they do not even know who the subjects are and what contexts they are working in. For the research goals of psychologists, this probably makes sense. But the research goals of the NLG community are different from the research goals of the psychological community; should we place more emphasis on ecological validity than they do, and less on control?

My own opinions on this matter are changing. Five years ago, I would have echoed the feeling that control is all-important. Now, though, I am beginning to think that in order to achieve both NLG's scientific goals (understanding language and computation) and NLG's technological goals (developing useful real-world technology), we need to put more emphasis on ecological validity in our evaluations.

2 Evaluation which is both controlled and in real-world context: STOP and DIAG

An ideal evaluation is one which is both controlled and done in a real-world context. An example is the evaluation of the STOP system. which generated tailored smoking-cessation advice based on the user's response to a questionnaire (Lennox et al., 2001; Reiter et al., 2003). The STOP project was a collaboration with medical colleagues, and the STOP evaluation (which was designed by the medics) was carried out as a randomised controlled clinical trial. We recruited 2500 smokers, and sent one-third of them STOP letters, one-third a non-tailored (canned) letter, and one-third a letter which just thanked them for being in out study. After 6 months we asked participants if they had stopped smoking; we tested saliva samples from people who said they had quit in order to verify their smoking status. The result of this evaluation was that the STOP tailored letters were no more effective than the control non-tailored letter. The STOP evaluation cost about UK£75,000, and took about 20 months to design, organise, and carry out.

The STOP evaluation was carried out in a real-world context; the letters were sent to actual smokers, and we measured whether they quit smoking. It was also controlled, since the impact of STOP letters was compared to the impact of non-tailored letters. However there was a lot of 'noise' (in the statistical sense) in the STOP evaluation, because different people (with different personalities, attitudes towards smoking, personal circumstances, etc) received the tailored and non-tailored letters, and this impacted smoking-cessation rates in the the three groups.

Another evaluation which was controlled and was done at least partially in a real-world context was the evaluation of the DIAG-NLP intelligent tutoring system (di Eugenio et al., 2005). In this experiment, 75 students (the appropriate subject group for this tutoring system) were divided into three groups: two groups interacted with two versions of the DIAG-NLP system, and a third interacted with a control version of DIAG which did not include any NLG. Effectiveness was measured by learning gain (change in knowledge, measured by differences in scores in a pre-test and post-test), which is standard in the tutoring system domain. The evaluation showed that students learned more from the second (more advanced) version of the DIAG-NLP system than from the non-NLG version of DIAG.

The DIAG-NLP evaluation was controlled, and it was real-world in the sense that it used representative subjects and measured real-world outcome. However, it appears (the paper is not completely explicit about this) that the evaluation assessed learning about a topic (fixing a home heating system) which was not part of the student's normal curriculum; if this is the case, then the evaluation was not 100% in a real-world context.

3 Evaluation which is controlled but not real-world: BT-45 and Young (1999)

The Babytalk project (Gatt et al., 2009) developed several NLG systems which summarised clinical data from babies in neonatal intensive care (NICU), for different audiences and purposes; one of these systems, BT45 (Portet et al., 2009), summarised 45 minutes of data for doctors and nurses, to support immediate decision-making. Babytalk was a collaborative project with clinical staff and psychologists, and the psychologists designed the BT45 evaluation (van der Meulen et al., 2010).

We picked 24 data sets (scenarios) based on historical data from babies who had been in NICU 5 years previously, and for each data set created three presentations: visualisation, computer-generated text, and human-written text. For each data set, we also asked expert consultants what actions should be taken by medical staff. We then asked 35 medical staff (doctors and nurses of varied expertise levels) to look at the scenarios using a mix of presentations, in a Latin Square design; eg, 1/3 of the subjects saw the visualisation of scenario 1 data, 1/3 saw the computer-generated summary of scenario 1 data, and 1/3 saw the human-written summary of this data. Also each subject saw the same number of scenarios in each condition, this reduced the impact of individual differences between subjects. Subjects were asked to make decisions about appropriate medical actions (or say no action should be taken), and responses were compared to the 'gold standard' recommendations from the consultants. The result was that decision performance was best with the human-written summaries; there was no significant difference between overall decision performance with the computer-generated summaries and the visualisation (although at the level of individual scenarios, computer texts were more effective in some scenarios, and visualisations was more effective in other scenarios). The BT45 evaluation cost about UK£20,000, and took about 6 months to design, organise, and carry out.

The BT45 evaluation was carefully controlled However, it was not done in a real-world context. Doctors and nurses sat in an experiment room (not in the ward) and looked at data from babies they did not remember (as opposed to babies whom they knew well because they has been looking after them for the past few weeks); they also did not visually observe the babies, which is a very important information source for NICU staff.

Many other task-based evaluations of NLG systems have been controlled but not done in a real-world context, including the very first task-based NLG evaluation I am aware of, by Young (1999). Young developed four algorithms for generating instructional texts, and tested these by asking 26 students to follow the instructions generated by the various algorithms on several scenarios, and measured error rates in carrying out the instructions. The instructions involved carrying out actions on campus (going to labs, playing in soccer matches, etc). The students did not actually carry out these actions, instead they interacted with a 'text-based virtual reality system'. Hence the evaluation was controlled but not carried out in real-world context.

4 Evaluation which is real-world but not controlled: BT-Nurse

The next Babytalk system (after BT45) was BT-NURSE; it generated summaries of 12-hours of clinical data, to support nursing shift handover (Hunter et al., 2011). We initially expected to evaluate BT-NURSE using a similar methodology to the BT45 evaluation. However the medical people involved in BabyTalk complained that it was unrealistic to evaluate the system in an artificial controlled context, where clinical staff were looking at data out of context. So instead we evaluated BT-NURSE by installing the system in the NICU, so that nurses used it to get information about babies they were actually caring for. The primary outcome measure was subjective ratings by nurses as to the helpfulness of BT-NURSE texts; and indeed most nurses thought the texts were helpful.

The BT-NURSE evaluation was significantly more expensive than the BT45 evaluation, because we hired a full-time software engineer for a year to ensure that the software was sufficiently well engineered so that it could be deployed and used in the hospital; we were also required by the medical ethics committee to have a research nurse on-site who checked texts for errors before they were shown to the duty nurses, and removed them from the experiment if they were factually incorrect and could damage patient care (in fact this never happened, the research nurse did not regard any of the BT-NURSE texts as potentially harmful from this perspective). All in all cost was probably about UK£50,000, and the entire process (including the software engineering) took about 18 months.

The BT-NURSE evaluation was not controlled; we did not compare the computer generated texts to anything else, and indeed did not directly measure any task outcome variable, instead we solicited opinions as to utility. It was however ecologically valid, since it was carried out by asking nurses (real-world users) to use BT-NURSE for care planning (real-world task) in a real-world context (on-ward, involving babies the nurses were familiar with and could visually observe).

5 Discussion

Ideally a task-based evaluation should be both controlled and ecologically valid (done in a real-world context). But if it is not possible to achieve both of these objectives, which is most important? Obviously in many cases the desires of collaborators need to be considered; for example psychologists generally place much more emphasis on control than on ecological validity, whereas many commercial organisation take the opposite perspective. But which is more important from an NLG perspective?

From a pragmatic perspective, two important arguments for focusing on control are cost and publications. The figures given above suggest that doing an evaluation in a real-world context makes it substantially more expensive. Of course this is based on very limited data, but I believe this is correct, deploying a system in a real-world context requires addressing engineering and ethical issues which are expensive and time-consuming to resolve. From a publications perspective; most NLG reviewers are much more concerned about control than about ecological validity. Especially in high-prestige venues, reviewers are likely to complain about uncontrolled evaluations, while making little (if any) mention of concerns about lack of ecological validity.

For what its worth, my own view on this issue has changed. If asked five years ago, I would have said that control was more important, but now I am veering more towards ecological validity. The technological goal of NLG is to develop technology which is used in real-world applications, and from this perspective if we do not evaluate in real-world contexts, we risk being side-tracked into technology which looks good in a controlled environment but is useless in the real world. Similarly, if our goal is to develop a better scientific understanding of computation and language, I think we have to look at how language is used in real-world contexts, which (at least in my mind) is quite different from how language is used in artificial contexts.

Plaisant (2004) made some related points in her discussion of evaluation of information visualisation. She pointed out that controlled evaluations of visualisation systems in artificial contexts might be less informative than uncontrolled evaluations in real-world contexts. She also pointed out that controlled evaluations could not evaluate some of the most important benefits of visualisation systems. For example, sometimes the primary objective of visualisation systems is to support scientific discovery, that is to make it easier for scientists who are analysing data to come up with new insights and hypotheses. However, testing effectiveness at supporting scientific discovery in a controlled fashion is almost impossible. Perhaps in theory one could compare the 'productivity' of two groups of scientists, one with and one without visualisation tools, but the comparison would have to involve a large number of scientists over a period of months or even years, with scientists in one group not allowed to communicate with scientists in the other group. It is difficult to imagine that such an experiment could in fact be carried out (or that it would be approved by a research ethics committee). Plaisant argues that focusing on controlled experiments means focusing on things that are easily measurable in such experiments, which may lead researchers to ignore the outcomes that we really care about.

Another important point is that the goal of evaluation is not just to assess if something works, but also to come up with insights as to how to improve an algorithm, module, or system. In NLG evaluations such insights are often based on free-text comments made by subjects, and in my experience better and more insightful comments are obtained from evaluations in real-world contexts.

An important potential caveat is that all of the examples cited above were system evaluations, which attempted to assess how useful a system was from an applied perspective. If the goal of an evaluation is to test a scientific theory or model, should we always (as psychologists do) favour control over ecological validity? My own belief is that the psychologists are missing important insights and findings by ignoring ecological validity, and the most effective way for the NLG community to 'add value' to the enterprise of understanding language is not to imitate the psychologists, but rather to use a different experimental paradigm, which focuses much more on ecological validity. But others will no doubt disagree.

6 Conclusion

It is difficult to choose between control and ecological validity, because clearly both greatly contribute to the usefulness of an evaluation. But this tradeoff must be made in many cases, and it would be preferable for it to be explicitly discussed. And of course there are many other desirable factors which may need to be involved in a tradeoff; for example, how important is it that subjects be representative of the user community, instead of whoever is easiest to recruit (eg, undergraduates). My hope is that the NLG community can explicitly discuss such issues, and come up with recommended evaluation methodologies for task-based studies, which are based the scientific and technological objectives of our community.

References

Barbara di Eugenio, Davide Fossati, Dan Yu, Susan Haller, and Michael Glass. 2005. Aggregation improves learning: experiments in natural language generation for intelligent tutoring systems. In *Proceedings of the 43rd Annual Meeting on Association for Computational Linguistics*, pages 50–57. Association for Computational Linguistics.

Albert Gatt, Francois Portet, Ehud Reiter, Jum Hunter, Saad Mahamood, Wendy Moncur, and Somayajulu Sripada. 2009. From data to text in the neonatal intensive care unit: Using NLG technology for decision support and information management. *AI Communications*, 22(3):153–186.

James Hunter, Yvonne Freer, Albert Gatt, Ehud Reiter, Somayajulu Sripada, Cindy Sykes, and Dave Westwater. 2011. BT-Nurse: Computer generation of natural language shift summaries from complex heterogeneous medical data. *Journal of the Americal Medical Informatics Association*. In press.

Scott Lennox, Liesl Osman, Ehud Reiter, Roma Robertson, James Friend, Ian McCann, Diane Skatun, and Peter Donnan. 2001. The cost-effectiveness of computer-tailored and non-tailored smoking cessation letters in general practice: A randomised controlled study. *British Medical Journal*, 322:1396–1400.

Catherine Plaisant. 2004. The challenge of information visualization evaluation. In *Proceedings of Advanced Visual Interfaces (AVI) 2004*.

François Portet, Ehud Reiter, Albert Gatt, Jim Hunter, Somayajulu Sripada, Yvonne Freer, and Cindy Sykes. 2009. Automatic generation of textual summaries from neonatal intensive care data. *Artificial Intelligence*, 173(7-8):789–816.

Ehud Reiter, Roma Robertson, and Liesl Osman. 2003. Lessons from a failure: Generating tailored smoking cessation letters. *Artificial Intelligence*, 144:41–58.

Marianne van der Meulen, Robert Logie, Yvonne Freer, Cindy Sykes, Neil McIntosh, and Jim Hunter. 2010. When a graph is poorer than 100 words: A comparison of computerised natural language generation, human generated descriptions and graphical displays in neonatal intensive care. *Applied Cognitive Psychology*, 24(1):77–89.

Michael Young. 1999. Using Grice's maxim of quantity to select the content of plan descriptions. *Artificial Intelligence*, 115:215–256.

Exploring linguistically-rich patterns for question generation

Sérgio Curto
L^{2}F/INESC-ID Lisbon
sslc@l2f.inesc-id.pt

Ana Cristina Mendes
L^{2}F/INESC-ID Lisbon
IST, Tech. Univ. Lisbon
acbm@l2f.inesc-id.pt

Luísa Coheur
L^{2}F/INESC-ID Lisbon
IST, Tech. Univ. Lisbon
lcoheur@inesc-id.pt

Abstract

Linguistic patterns reflect the regularities of Natural Language and their applicability is acknowledged in several Natural Language Processing tasks. Particularly, in the task of Question Generation, many systems depend on patterns to generate questions from text. The approach we follow relies on patterns that convey lexical, syntactic and semantic information, automatically learned from large-scale corpora.

In this paper we discuss the impact of varying several parameters during pattern learning and matching in the Question Generation task. In particular, we introduce semantics (by means of named entities) in our lexico-syntactic patterns. We evaluate and compare the number and quality of the learned patterns and the matched text segments. Also, we detail the influence of the patterns in the generation of natural language questions.

1 Introduction

Natural Language (NL) is known for its variability and expressiveness. There are hundreds of ways to express an idea, to describe a fact. But language also comprises several regularities, or patterns, that denote the presence of certain information. For example, *Paris is located in France* is a common way to say that Paris is in France, indicated by the words *located in*.

The use of patterns is a widely accepted as an effective approach in the field of Natural Language Processing (NLP), in tasks like Question-Answering (QA) (Soubbotin, 2001; Ravichandran and Hovy, 2002) or Question Generation (QG) (Wyse and Piwek, 2009; Mendes et al., 2011).

Particularly, QG aims at generating questions from text and has became a vibrant line of research. Generating questions (and answers), on one hand, allows QA or Dialogue Systems to be easily ported to different domains, by quickly providing new questions to train the systems. On the other hand, it is useful for knowledge assessment-related tasks, by reducing the amount of time allocated for the creation of tests by teachers (a time consuming and tedious task if done manually), or by allowing the self evaluation of knowledge acquired by learners.

Most systems dedicated to QG are based on hand-crafted rules and rely on pattern matching to generate questions. For example, in (Chen et al., 2009), after the identification of key points, a situation model is built and question templates are used to generate questions. The Ceist system (Wyse and Piwek, 2009) uses syntactic patterns and the Tregex tool (Levy and Andrew, 2006) that receives a set of hand-crafted rules and matches the rules against parsed text, generating, in this way, questions (and answers). Kalady et al.(2010) bases the QG task in Up-keys (significant phrases in documents), parse tree manipulation and named entity recognition.

Our approach to QG also relies on linguistic patterns, defined as a sequence of symbols that convey lexical, syntactic and semantic information, reflecting and expressing a regularity of the language. The patterns associate a question to its answer and are automatically learned from a set of seeds, based on large-scale information corpora, shallow parsing and named entities recognition. The generation of questions uses the learned patterns, as questions are created from text segments found in free text after being matched against the patterns.

This paper studies the impact on QG of varying linguistic parameters during pattern learning and matching. It is organized as follows: in Sec. 2 we introduce our pattern-based approach to QG; in Sec. 3 we show the experiments and discuss results; in Sec. 4 we conclude and point to future work.

2 Linguistically-Rich Patterns for Question Generation

The generation of questions involves two phases: a first offline phase – *pattern learning* – where patterns are learned from a set of seeds; and a second online phase – *pattern matching and question generation* – where the learned patterns are matched against a target document and the questions are generated. Next we describe these phases.

Pattern Learning Our approach to pattern learning is inspired by the work of Ravichandran and Hovy (2002), who propose a method to learn patterns based on a two-step technique: the first acquires patterns from the Web given a set of seeds and the second validates the patterns. Despite the similarities, ours and Ravichandran and Hovy's work have some differences: our patterns also contain syntactic and semantic information and are not validated. Moreover, our seeds are well formulated NL questions and their respective correct answers (instead of two entities), which allows to directly take advantage of the test sets already built and made available in evaluation campaigns for QA systems (like Text REtrieval Conference (TREC) or Cross Language Evaluation Forum (CLEF)).

We use a set of seeds, each composed by a NL question and its correct answer. We start by classifying each seed question into a semantic category, in order to discover the type of information these are seeking after: for example, the question *"Who painted the Birth of Venus ?"* asks for a person's name. Afterwards, we extract the phrase nodes of each seed question (excluding the Wh-phrase), enclose each in double quotes and submit them as a query to a search engine. For instance, given the seed *"Who painted the Birth of Venus ?"/Botticelli* and the syntactic structure of its question [$_{\text{WHNP}}$ Who] [$_{\text{VBD}}$ painted] [$_{\text{NP}}$ the Birth of Venus][1], we build the query: `"painted" "the Birth of Venus" "Botticelli"`.

We build patterns that associate the entities in the question to the answer from the top retrieved documents. From the sentence *The Birth of Venus was painted around 1486 by Botticelli*, retrieved as result to the above query, we learn the pattern "`NP VBD[was] VBN PP[around 1486]:`*`[Date]`* `IN:[by] NP{`*`ANSWER`*`}`"[2]. The syntactic labels without lexical information are related with the constituents of the question, while those with "{*`ANSWER`*}" mark the answer.

By creating queries with the inflected forms of the main verb of the question, we learn patterns where the surface form of the verb is different to that of the verb in the seed question (*e.g.*, "`NP{`*`ANSWER`*`} VBD[began] VBG NP`" is learned from the sentence *Botticelli began painting the Birth of Venus*). The patterns generated by verb inflection are INFLECTED; the others are STRONG patterns.

Our patterns convey linguistic information extracted from the sentences in the documents where all the constituents of the query exist. The pattern is built with the words, their syntactic and semantic classes, that constitute the segments where those constituents are found. For that, we perform syntactic analysis and named entity recognition in each sentence. In this paper, we address the impact of adding semantic information to the patterns, that is, the difference in having a pattern "`NP VBD[was]` *`VBN`* `PP[around 1486]:`*`[Date]`* `IN:[by] NP{`*`ANSWER`*`}`" with or without the named entity of type DATE, for instance.

Pattern Matching and Question Generation The match of the patterns against a given free text is done at the lexical, syntactic and semantic levels. We have implemented a (recursive) algorithm that explores the parsed tree of the text sentences in a top-down, left-to-right, depth-first search, unifying the text with the linguistic information in the pattern.

Also, we discard all matched segments in which the answer does not agree with the semantic category expected by the question.

The generation of questions from the matched text

[1]The Penn Treebank II Tags (Bies et al., 1995) are used.

[2]The patterns are more complex than the ones presented: they are linked to the seed question by indexes, mapping the position of each of its components into the question constituents.

segments is straightforward, since we keep track of the syntactic structure of the questions and the sentences on the origin of the patterns. There is a direct unification of all components of the text segment with the constituents of the pattern. In the INFLECTED patterns, the verb is inflected with the tense and person of the seed question and the auxiliary verb is also used.

3 Experiments

3.1 Experimental Setup

We used the 6 seeds shown in Table 1, chosen because the questions contain regular verbs and they focus on known entities – being so, it is probable that there will be several texts in the Web referring to them. However, understanding the characteristics of a pair that makes it a good seed is an important and pertinent question and a direction for future work.

GId: 1 **Syntactic Structure:** WHNP VBD NP **Semantic Category:** HUMAN:INDIVIDUAL
"Who wrote Hamlet?"/Shakespeare *"Who painted Guernica?"/Picasso* *"Who painted The Starry Night?"/Van Gogh*
GId: 2 **Syntactic Structure:** WHADVP VBD NP VBN **Semantic Category:** NUMERIC:DATE
"When was Hamlet written?"/1601 *"When was Guernica painted?"/1937* *"When was The Starry Night painted?"/1889*

Table 1: Seeds used in the experiments.

The syntactic analysis of the questions was done by the Berkeley Parser (Petrov and Klein, 2007) trained on the QuestionBank (Judge et al., 2006). For question classification, we used Li and Roth (2002) taxonomy and a machine learning-based classifier fed with features derived from a rule-based classifier (Silva et al., 2011).

For the learning of patterns we used the top 64 documents retrieved by Google and to recognize the named entities in the pattern we apply several strategies, namely: 1) the Stanford's Conditional Random-Field-based named entity recognizer (Finkel et al., 2005) to detect entities of type HUMAN; 2) regular expressions to detect NUMERIC and DATE type entities; 3) gazetteers to detect entities of type LOCATION.

For the generation of questions we used the top 16 documents retrieved by the Google for 9 personalities from several domains, like literature (*e.g.*, Jane Austen) and politics (*e.g.*, Adolf Hitler). We do not have influence on the content of the retrieved documents, nor perform any pre-processing (like text simplification or anaphora resolution). The Berkeley Parser (Petrov and Klein, 2007) was used to parse the sentences, trained with the Wall Street Journal.

3.2 Pattern Learning Results

A total of 272 patterns was learned, from which 212 are INFLECTED and the remaining are STRONG. On average, each seed led to 46 patterns.

Table 2 shows the number of learned patterns of types INFLECTED and STRONG according to each group of seed questions. It indicates the number of patterns in which at least one named entity was recognized (W) and the number of patterns which do not contain any named entity (WO). Three main results of the pattern learning phase are shown: 1) the number of learned INFLECTED patterns is much higher than the number of learned STRONG patterns: nearly 80% of the patterns are INFLECTED; 2) most of the patterns do not have named entities; and 3) the number of patterns learned from the questions of group 1 are nearly 70% of the total number of patterns.

	INFLECTED		STRONG		
GId	WO	W	WO	W	TOTAL
1	127	19	36	8	
	146		44		190
2	40	26	10	6	
	66		16		82
All	167	45	46	14	
	212		60		272

Table 2: Number of learned patterns.

The following are examples of patterns and the actual sentences from where they were learned:

– "`NP{ANSWER} VBZ NP`": an INFLECTED pattern learned from group 1, from the sentence *1601 William Shakespeare writes Hamlet in London.*, without named entities;

– "`NP VBD VBN IN[in] NP{ANSWER}`": a

STRONG pattern learned from group 2, from the sentence *(Guernica was painted in 1937.)*, without named entities;

– "NNP VBZ[is] NP[a tragedy] ,[,] VBN[believed] VBN IN[between] NP[1599]: *[NUMERIC_COUNT, NUMERIC_DATE]* CC[and] NP{ANSWER}": an INFLECTED pattern learned from group 2, from the sentence *William Shakespeare's Hamlet is a tragedy , believed written between 1599 and 1601*, with 1599 being recognized as named entity of type NUMERIC_COUNT and NUMERIC_DATE.

3.3 Pattern Matching and Question Generation Results

Regarding the number of text segments matched in the texts retrieved for the 9 personalities, Table 3 shows that, from the 272 learned patterns, only 30 (11%) were in fact effective (an effective pattern matches at least one text segment). The most effective patterns were those from group 2, as 12 from 82 (14.6%) matched at least one instance in the text.

GId	INFLECTED	STRONG	TOTAL
1	13	5	18
2	9	3 (2 W)	12
All	22	8	30

Table 3: Matched patterns.

Regarding the patterns with named entities, only those from group 2 matched instances in the texts. The pattern that matched the most instances was "NP{ANSWER} VBD NP", learned from group 1.

In the evaluation of the questions, we use the guidelines of Chen et al. (2009), who classify questions as *plausible* – if they are grammatically correct and if they make sense regarding the text from where they were extracted – and *implausible* (otherwise).

However, we split plausible questions in three categories: 1) P_a for plausible, anaphoric questions, *e.g.*, *When was she awarded the Nobel Peace Prize?*; 2) P_c for plausible questions that need a context to be answered, *e.g.*, *When was the manuscript published?*; and 3) P_p, a plausible perfect question. If a question can be marked both as PL_a and PL_c, we mark it as PL_a. Also, we split implausible questions in: 1) IP_i: for implausible questions due to incompleteness, *e.g.*, *When was Bob Marley invited?*; and 2) IP: for questions that make no sense, *e.g.*, *When was December 1926 Agatha identified?*.

A total of 447 questions was generated: 31 by STRONG patterns, 269 by INFLECTED patterns and 147 by both STRONG and INFLECTED patterns. We manually evaluated 100 questions, randomly selected. Results are in Table 4, shown according to the type (INFLECTED/STRONG) and presence of named entities (W/WO) in the pattern that generated them.

	P_a	P_c	P_p	IP_i	IP	Total
INFLECTED						57
WO	2	0	27	23	5	
STRONG						13
W	**1**	0	**1**	0	**1**	
WO	1	2	3	3	1	
INFL/STR						30
WO	0	0	9	18	3	
All	4	2	40	44	10	100

Table 4: Evaluation of the generated questions.

46 of the evaluated questions were considered plausible and, from these, 40 can be used without modifications. From the 54 implausible questions, 44 were due to lack of information in the question. 69% (9 in 13) of the questions originated in STRONG patterns were plausible. This value is smaller for questions generated by INFLECTED patterns: 50.8% (29 in 57). Questions that had in their origin both a STRONG and a INFLECTED pattern were mostly implausible, only 9 in 30 were plausible (30%). The presence of named entities led to an increase of questions of only 3 (2 plausible and 1 implausible).

3.4 Discussion

The results concerning the transition from lexico-syntactic to lexico-syntactic-semantic patterns were not conclusive. There were 59 patterns with named entities, but only 2 matched new text segments. Only 3 questions were generated from patterns with semantics. We think that this happened due to two reasons: 1) not all of the named entities in the patterns were detected; and 2) the patterns contained lexical information that did not allow a match with the text (*e.g.*, "NP{ANSWER} VBD[responded]

`PP[in 1937]:textit[Date] WHADVP[when] NP[he] VBD NP`" requires the words *responded*, *when* and *he*.)

From a small set of seeds, our approach learned patterns that were later used to generate 447 questions from previously unseen text. In a sample of 100 questions, 46% were judged as plausible. Two plausible questions are: *"Who had no real interest in the former German African colonies?"*, *"When was The Road to Resurgence published?"* and *"Who launched a massive naval and land campaign designed to seize New York?"*.

The presence of syntactic information (a difference between ours and Ravichandran and Hovy's work) allows to relax the patterns and to generate questions of various topics: *e.g.*, the questions *"Who invented the telegraph?"* and *"Who directed the Titanic?"* can be generated from matching the pattern "`NP VBD[was] VBN IN:[by] NP{ANSWER}`" with the sentences *The telegraph was invented by Samuel Morse* and *The Titanic was directed by James Cameron*, respectively.

4 Conclusions and Future Work

We presented an approach to generating questions based on linguistic patterns, automatically learned from the Web from a set of seeds. We addressed the impact of adding semantics to patterns in matching text segments and generating new NL questions.

We did not detect any improvement when adding semantics to the patterns, mostly because the patterns with named entities did not match too many text segments. Nevertheless, from a small set of 6 seeds, we generated 447 NL questions. From these, we evaluated 100 and 46% were considered correct at the lexical, syntactic and semantic levels.

In the future, we intend to pre-process the texts against which the patterns are matched and from which the questions are generated. Also, we are experimenting this approach in another language. We aim at using more complex questions as seeds, studying its influence on the generation of questions.

Acknowledgements

This work was supported by FCT (INESC-ID multiannual funding) through the PIDDAC Program funds, and also through the project FALACOMIGO (ProjectoVII em co-promoção, QREN n 13449).

Ana Cristina Mendes is supported by a PhD fellowship from Fundação para a Ciência e a Tecnologia (SFRH/BD/43487/2008).

References

Ann Bies, Mark Ferguson, Karen Katz, and Robert Macintyre. 1995. Bracketing Guidelines for Treebank II Style Penn Treebank Project.

Wei Chen, Gregory Aist, , and Jack Mostow. 2009. Generating questions automatically from informational text. In *The 2nd Workshop on Question Generation.*

Jenny Rose Finkel, Trond Grenager, and Christopher Manning. 2005. Incorporating non-local information into information extraction systems by gibbs sampling. In *Proc. 43rd Annual Meeting on Association for Computational Linguistics*, ACL '05, pages 363–370. ACL.

John Judge, Aoife Cahill, and Josef van Genabith. 2006. Questionbank: creating a corpus of parse-annotated questions. In *ACL-44: Proc. 21st Int. Conf. on Computational Linguistics and the 44th Annual Meeting of the Association for Computational Linguistics*, pages 497–504. ACL.

Saidalavi Kalady, Ajeesh Elikkottil, and Rajarshi Das. 2010. Natural language question generation using syntax and keywords. In *The 3rd Workshop on Question Generation.*

Roger Levy and Galen Andrew. 2006. Tregex and tsurgeon: tools for querying and manipulating tree data structures. In *LREC 2006.*

Xin Li and Dan Roth. 2002. Learning question classifiers. In *Proc. 19th Int. Conf. on Computational Linguistics*, pages 1–7. ACL.

Ana Cristina Mendes, Sérgio Curto, and Luísa Coheur. 2011. Bootstrapping multiple-choice tests with thementor. In *CICLing, 12th International Conference on Intelligent Text Processing and Computational Linguistics.*

Slav Petrov and Dan Klein. 2007. Improved inference for unlexicalized parsing. In *Human Language Technologies 2007: The Conference of the North American Chapter of the Association for Computational Linguistics; Proc. Main Conference*, pages 404–411. ACL.

Deepak Ravichandran and Eduard Hovy. 2002. Learning surface text patterns for a question answering system. In *ACL '02: Proc. 40th Annual Meeting on Association for Computational Linguistics*, pages 41–47. ACL.

João Silva, Luísa Coheur, Ana Mendes, and Andreas Wichert. 2011. From symbolic to sub-symbolic information in question classification. *Artificial Intelligence Review*, 35:137–154.

M. M. Soubbotin. 2001. Patterns of potential answer expressions as clues to the right answers. In *Proc. 10th Text REtrieval Conference (TREC)*, pages 293–302.

Brendan Wyse and Paul Piwek. 2009. Generating questions from openlearn study units. In *The 2nd Workshop on Question Generation*.

Linguistically Motivated Complementizer Choice in Surface Realization

Rajakrishnan Rajkumar and **Michael White**
Department of Linguistics
The Ohio State University
Columbus, OH, USA
{raja,mwhite}@ling.osu.edu

Abstract

This paper shows that using linguistically motivated features for English *that*-complementizer choice in an averaged perceptron model for classification can improve upon the prediction accuracy of a state-of-the-art realization ranking model. We report results on a binary classification task for predicting the presence/absence of a *that*-complementizer using features adapted from Jaeger's (2010) investigation of the uniform information density principle in the context of *that*-mentioning. Our experiments confirm the efficacy of the features based on Jaeger's work, including information density–based features. The experiments also show that the improvements in prediction accuracy apply to cases in which the presence of a *that*-complementizer arguably makes a substantial difference to fluency or intelligiblity. Our ultimate goal is to improve the performance of a ranking model for surface realization, and to this end we conclude with a discussion of how we plan to combine the local complementizer-choice features with those in the global ranking model.

1 Introduction

Johnson (2009) observes that in developing statistical parsing models, "shotgun" features — that is, myriad scattershot features that pay attention to superficial aspects of structure — tend to be remarkably useful, while features based on linguistic theory seem to be of more questionable utility, with the most basic linguistic insights tending to have the greatest impact.[1] Johnson also notes that feature design is perhaps the most important but least understood aspect of statistical parsing, and thus the disappointing impact of linguistic theory on parsing models is of real consequence. In this paper, by contrast, we show that in the context of surface realization, using linguistically motivated features for English *that*-complementizer choice can improve upon the prediction accuracy of a state-of-the-art realization ranking model, arguably in ways that make a substantial difference to fluency and intelligiblity.[2] In particular, we report results on a binary classification task for predicting the presence or absence of a *that*-complementizer using features adapted from Jaeger's (2010) investigation of the **uniform information density** principle in the context of *that*-mentioning. This information-theoretic principle predicts that language production is affected by a preference to distribute information uniformly across the linguistic signal. In Jaeger's study, uniform information density emerges as an important predictor of speakers' syntactic reduction preferences even when taking a sizeable variety of controls based on competing hypotheses into account. Our experiments confirm the efficacy of the features based on Jaeger's work, including information density–based features.

[1]The term *"shotgun" feature* appears in the slides for Johnson's talk (`http://www.cog.brown.edu/~mj/papers/johnson-eacl09-workshop.pdf`), rather than in the paper itself.

[2]For German surface realization, Cahill and Riester (2009) show that incorporating information status features based on the linguistics literature improves performance on realization ranking.

That-complementizers are optional words that introduce sentential complements in English. In the Penn Treebank, they are left out roughly two-thirds of the time, thereby enhancing conciseness. This follows the low complementizer rates reported in previous work (Tagliamonte and Smith, 2005; Cacoullos and Walker, 2009). While some surface realizers, such as FUF/SURGE (Elhadad, 1991), have made use of input features to control the choice of whether to include a *that*-complementizer, for many applications the decision seems best left to the realizer, since multiple surface syntactic factors appear to govern the choice, rather than semantic ones. In our experiments, we use the OpenCCG[3] surface realizer with logical form inputs underspecified for the presence of *that* in complement clauses. While in many cases, adding or removing *that* results in an acceptable paraphrase, in the following example, the absence of *that* in (2) introduces a local ambiguity, which the original Penn Treebank sentence avoids by including the complementizer.

(1) He said that for the second month in a row, food processors reported a shortage of nonfat dry milk. (WSJ0036.61)

(2) ? He said for the second month in a row, food processors reported a shortage of nonfat dry milk.

The starting point for this paper is White and Rajkumar's (2009) realization ranking model, a state-of-the-art model employing shotgun features galore. An error analysis of this model, performed by comparing CCGbank Section 00 realized derivations with their corresponding gold standard derivations, revealed that out of a total of 543 *that*-complementizer cases, the realized output did not match the gold standard choice 82 times (see Table 3 in Section 5 for details). Most of these mismatches involved cases where a clause originally containing a *that*-complementizer was realized in reduced form, with no *that*. This under-prediction of *that*-inclusion is not surprising, since the realization ranking model makes use of baseline n-gram model features, and n-gram models are known to have a built-in bias for strings with fewer words.

[3]openccg.sf.net

We report here on experiments comparing this global model to ones that employ local features specifically designed for *that*-choice in complement clauses. As a prelude to incorporating these features into a model for realization ranking, we study the efficacy of these features in isolation by means of a binary classification task to predict the presence/absence of *that* in complement clauses. In a global realization ranking setting, the impact of these phenomenon-specific features might be less evident, as they would interact with other features for lexical selection and ordering choices that the ranker makes. Note that a comprehensive ranking model is desirable, since linear ordering and *that*-complementizer choices may interact. For example, Hawkins (2003) reports examples where explicitly marked phrases can occur either close to or far from their heads as in (3) and (4), whereas zero-marked phrases are only rarely attested at some distance from their heads and prefer adjacency, as (5) and (6) show.

(3) I realized [that he had done it] with sadness in my heart.

(4) I realized with sadness in my heart [that he had done it].

(5) I realized [he had done it] with sadness in my heart.

(6) ? I realized with sadness in my heart [he had done it].

2 Background

CCG (Steedman, 2000) is a unification-based categorial grammar formalism defined almost entirely in terms of lexical entries that encode subcategorization as well as syntactic features (e.g. number and agreement). OpenCCG is a parsing/generation library which includes a hybrid symbolic-statistical chart realizer (White, 2006). The chart realizer takes as input logical forms represented internally using Hybrid Logic Dependency Semantics (HLDS), a dependency-based approach to representing linguistic meaning (Baldridge and Kruijff, 2002). To illustrate the input to OpenCCG, consider the semantic dependency graph in Figure 1. In the graph, each node has a lexical predication (e.g. **make.03**) and a set of semantic features (e.g.

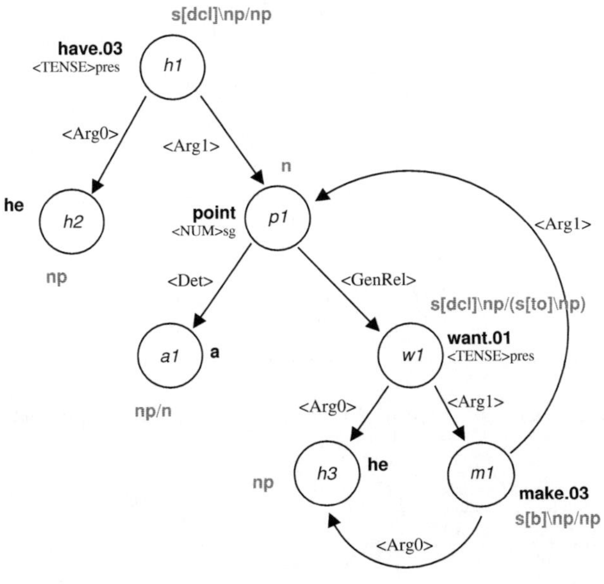

Figure 1: Semantic dependency graph from the CCGbank for *He has a point he wants to make [. . .]*, along with gold-standard supertags (category labels)

⟨NUM⟩sg); nodes are connected via dependency relations (e.g. ⟨ARG0⟩). In HLDS, each semantic head (corresponding to a node in the graph) is associated with a nominal that identifies its discourse referent, and relations between heads and their dependents are modeled as modal relations. We extract HLDS-based quasi logical form graphs from the CCG-bank and semantically empty function words such as complementizers, infinitival-*to*, expletive subjects, and case-marking prepositions are adjusted to reflect their purely syntactic status. Alternative realizations are ranked using an averaged perceptron model described in the next section.

3 Feature Design

White and Rajkumar's (2009) realization ranking model serves as the baseline for this paper. It is a global, averaged perceptron ranking model using three kinds of features: (1) the log probability of the candidate realization's word sequence according to three linearly interpolated language models (as well as a feature for each component model), much as in the log-linear models of Velldal & Oepen (2005) and Nakanishi et al. (2005); (2) integer-valued syntactic features, representing counts of occurrences in a derivation, from Clark & Curran's (2007) normal form model; and (3) discriminative n-gram features (Roark et al., 2004), which count the occurrences of each n-gram in the word sequence.

Table 1 shows the new complementizer-choice features investigated in this paper. The example features mentioned in the table are taken from the two complement clause (CC) forms (with-*that* CC vs. *that*-less CC) of the sentence below:

(7) The finding probably will support those who **argue** [*that*/∅ the U.S. should regulate the class of asbestos including crocidolite more stringently than the common kind of asbestos, chrysotile, found in most schools and other buildings], Dr. Talcott said. (WSJ0003.19)

The first class of features, dependency length and position of CC, have been adapted from the related control features in Jaeger's (2010) study. For the above example, the position of the matrix verb with respect to the start of the sentence (feature name *mvInd* and having the value 7.0), the distance between the matrix verb and the onset of the CC (feature name *mvCCDist* with the value 1.0) and finally the length of the CC (feature *ccLen* with value of 29.0 for the *that*-CC and 28.0 for the *that*-less CC) are encoded as features. The second class of features includes various properties of the matrix verb viz. POS tag, form, stem and supertag (feature names *mv Pos, mvStem, mvForm, mvSt*, respectively). These features were motivated by the fact that Jaeger controls for the per-verb bias of this construction, as attested in the earlier literature. The third class of features are related to information density. Jaeger (2010) estimates information density at the CC onset by using matrix verb subcategorization frequency. In our case, more like the n-gram features employed by Levy and Jaeger (2007), we used log probabilities from two existing n-gram models, viz. a trigram word model and trigram word model with semantic class replacement. For each CC, two features (one per language model) were extracted by calculating the average of the log probs of individual words from the beginning of the complement clause. In the *that*-CC version of the example above, local CC-features having the prefix *$uidCCMean* were calculated by averaging the individual log probs of the 3 words *that the U.S.* to get feature values of -0.8353556 and -2.0460036 per language model (see

Feature	Example for *that*-CCs	Example for *that*-less CCs
Dependency length and position of CC		
Position of matrix verb	thatCC:mvInd 7.0	noThatCC:mvInd 7.0
Dist between matrix verb & CC	thatCC:mvCCDist 1.0	noThatCC:mvCCDist 1.0
Length of CC	thatCC:ccLen 29.0	noThatCC:ccLen 28.0
Matrix verb features		
POS-tag	thatCC:mvPos:VBP 1.0	noThatCC:mvPos:VBP 1.0
Stem	thatCC:mvStem:argue 1.0	noThatCC:mvStem:argue 1.0
Form	thatCC:mvForm:argue 1.0	noThatCC:mvForm:argue 1.0
CCG supertag	thatCC:mvSt:s[dcl]\np/s[em] 1.0	noThatCC:mvSt:s[dcl]\np/s[dcl] 1.0
uniform information density (UID)		
Average n-gram log probs of first 2 words of *that-less* CCs or first 3 words of *that*-CCs	thatCC:$uidCCMean1 -0.8353556 thatCC:$uidCCMean2 -2.0460036	noThatCC:$uidCCMean1 -2.5177214 noThatCC:$uidCCMean2 -3.6464245

Table 1: New features introduced (the prefix of each feature encodes the type of CC; subsequent parts supply the feature name)

last part of Table 1). In the *that*-less CC version, *$uidCCMean* features were calculated by averaging the log probs of the first two words in the complement clause, i.e. *the U.S.*

4 Classification Experiment

To train a local classification model to predict the presence of *that* in complement clauses, we used an averaged perceptron ranking model with the complementizer-specific features listed in Table 1 to rank alternate with-*that* vs. *that*-less CC choices. For each CC classification instance in CCGbank Sections 02–21, the derivation of the competing alternate choice was created; i.e., in the case of a *that*-CC, the corresponding *that*-less CC was created and vice versa. Table 2 illustrates classification results on Sections 00 (development) using models containing different feature sets & Section 23 (final test) for the best-performing classification and ranking models. For both the development as well as test sections, the local classification model performed significantly better than the global realization ranking model according to McNemar's χ^2 test ($p = 0.005$, two-tailed). Feature ablation tests on the development data (Section 00) revealed that removing the information density features resulted in a loss of accuracy of around 1.8%.

5 Discussion

As noted in the introduction, in many cases, adding or removing *that* to/from the corpus sentence results in an acceptable paraphrase, while in other cases the presence of *that* appears to make a substantial difference to intelligibility or fluency. In order to better understand the effect of the complementizer-specific features, we examined three construction types in the development data, viz. non-adjacent complement clauses, gerundive matrix verbs and a host of sub-cases involving a matrix *be*-verb (*wh*-clefts, *be*+adjective etc.), where the presence of *that* seemed to make the most difference. The results are provided in Table 3. As is evident, the global realization ranking model under-proposes the *that*-choice, most likely due to the preference of n-gram models towards fewer words, while the local classifica-

Model Features	% 00	% 23
Most Frequent Baseline	68.7	66.8
Global Realization Ranking	78.45	77.0
Local That-*Classification*		
Only UID feats	74.77	
Table 1 features except UID ones	81.4	
Both feature sets above	**83.24**	**83.02**

Table 2: Classification accuracy results (Section 00 has 170/543 *that*-CCs; Section 23 has 192/579 *that*-CCs)

Construction	%*that*	% *that* / %Accuracy	
	Gold	Classification	Ranking
Gerundive (26)	53.8	61.5 / 92.3	26.9 / 57.7
Be-verb (21)	71.4	95.2 / 66.7	47.6 / 57.1
Non-adjacent CCs (53)	49.1	54.7 / 67.9	30.2 / 66.0
Total (543)	31.3	29.3 / 83.2	21.9 / 78.5

Table 3: Section 00 construction-wise *that*-CC proportions and model accuracies (total CC counts given in brackets alongside labels); gold standard obviously has 100% accuracy; models are local *that*-classification and White and Rajkumar's (2009) global realization ranking model

WSJ0049.64	**Observing** [*that*/?∅ the judge has never exhibited any bias or prejudice], Mr. Murray concluded that he would be impartial in any case involving a homosexual or prostitute as a victim.
WSJ0020.16	" what this tells us **is** [*that*/?∅ U.S. trade law is working] ", he said .
WSJ0010.5	The idea, of course: to **prove** to 125 corporate decision makers [*that*/?∅ the buckle on the Rust Belt is n't so rusty after all , that it 's a good place for a company to expand].
WSJ0044.118	Editorials in the Greenville newspaper **allowed** [that/?∅ Mrs. Yeargin was wrong], but also said the case showed how testing was being overused.
WSJ0060.7	Viacom **denies** [∅/?*that* it 's using pressure tactics].
WSJ0018.4	The documents also **said** [*that*/?∅ although the 64-year-old Mr. Cray has been working on the project for more than six years , the Cray-3 machine is at least another year away from a fully operational prototype].

Table 4: Examples from model comparison

tion model is closer to the gold standard in terms of *that*-choice proportions. For all the three construction types as well as overall, classifier performance was better than ranker performance. The difference in performance between the local classification and global ranking models in the case of gerundive matrix verbs is statistically significant according to the McNemar's χ^2 test (Bonferroni corrected, two tailed $p = 0.001$). The performance difference was not significant with the other two constructions, however, using only the cases in Section 00.

Table 4 lists relevant examples where the classification model's *that*-choice prediction matched the gold standard while a competing model's prediction did not. Example WSJ0049.64 is one such instance of classifier success involving a gerundive matrix verb (in contrast to the realization ranking model), Example WSJ0020.16 exemplifies success with a *wh*-cleft construction and Example WSJ0010.5 contains a non-adjacent CC. Apart from these construction-based analyses, examples like WSJ0044.118 indicate that the classification model prefers the *that*-CC choice in cases that substantially improve intelligiblity, as here the overt complementizer helps to avoid a local syntactic ambiguity where the *NP* in *allowed NP* is unlikely to be interpreted as the start of an *S*.

Finally, we also studied the effect of the uniform information density features by comparing the full classification model to a model without the UID features. The full classification model exhibited a trend towards significantly outperforming the ablated model (McNemar's $p = 0.10$, 2-tailed); more test data would be needed to establish significance conclusively. Examples are shown at the bottom of Table 4. In WSJ0060.7, the full classification model predicted a *that*-less clause (matching the gold standard), while the ablated classification model predicted a clause with *that*. In all such examples except one, the information density features helped the classification model avoid predicting *that*-inclusion when not necessary. Example WSJ0018.4 is the only instance where the best classification model differed in predicting the *that*-choice.

6 Conclusions and Future Work

In this paper, we have shown that using linguistically motivated features for English *that*-complementizer choice in a local classifier can improve upon the prediction accuracy of a state-of-the-art global realization ranking model employing myriad shotgun features, confirming the efficacy of features based on Jaeger's (2010) investigation of the uniform information density principle in the context of *that*-mentioning. Since *that*-complementizer choice interacts with other realization decisions, in future work we plan to investigate incorporating these features into the global realization ranking model. This move will require binning the real-valued features, as multiple complement clauses can appear in a single sentence. Should feature-level integration prove ineffective, we also plan to investigate alternative architectures, such as using the local classifier outputs as features in the global model.

Acknowledgements

This work was supported in part by NSF IIS-0812297 and by an allocation of computing time from the Ohio Supercomputer Center. Our thanks also to Florian Jaeger, William Schuler, Peter Culicover and the anonymous reviewers for helpful comments and discussion.

References

Jason Baldridge and Geert-Jan Kruijff. 2002. Coupling CCG and Hybrid Logic Dependency Semantics. In *Proc. ACL-02*.

Rena Torres Cacoullos and James A. Walker. 2009. On the persistence of grammar in discourse formulas: A variationist study of "that". *Linguistics*, 47(1):1–43.

Stephen Clark and James R. Curran. 2007. Wide-Coverage Efficient Statistical Parsing with CCG and Log-Linear Models. *Computational Linguistics*, 33(4):493–552.

Michael Elhadad. 1991. FUF: The universal unifier user manual version 5.0. Technical Report CUCS-038-91, Dept. of Computer Science, Columbia University.

John A. Hawkins. 2003. Why are zero-marked phrases close to their heads? In Günter Rohdenburg and Britta Mondorf, editors, *Determinants of Grammatical Variation in English*, Topics in English Linguistics 43. De Gruyter Mouton, Berlin.

T. Florian Jaeger. 2010. Redundancy and reduction: Speakers manage information density. *Cognitive Psychology*, 61(1):23–62, August.

Mark Johnson. 2009. How the statistical revolution changes (computational) linguistics. In *Proceedings of the EACL 2009 Workshop on the Interaction between Linguistics and Computational Linguistics: Virtuous, Vicious or Vacuous?*, pages 3–11, Athens, Greece, March. Association for Computational Linguistics.

Roger Levy and T. Florian Jaeger. 2007. Speakers optimize information density through syntactic reduction. *Advances in Neural Information Processing Systems*, 19:849.

Hiroko Nakanishi, Yusuke Miyao, and Jun'ichi Tsujii. 2005. Probabilistic methods for disambiguation of an HPSG-based chart generator. In *Proc. IWPT-05*.

Brian Roark, Murat Saraclar, Michael Collins, and Mark Johnson. 2004. Discriminative language modeling with conditional random fields and the perceptron algorithm. In *Proc. ACL-04*.

Mark Steedman. 2000. *The syntactic process*. MIT Press, Cambridge, MA, USA.

S. Tagliamonte and J. Smith. 2005. No momentary fancy! the zero 'complementizer' in English dialects. *English Language and Linguistics*, 9(2):289–309.

Erik Velldal and Stephan Oepen. 2005. Maximum entropy models for realization ranking. In *Proc. MT Summit X*.

Michael White and Rajakrishnan Rajkumar. 2009. Perceptron reranking for CCG realization. In *Proceedings of the 2009 Conference on Empirical Methods in Natural Language Processing*, pages 410–419, Singapore, August. Association for Computational Linguistics.

Michael White. 2006. Efficient Realization of Coordinate Structures in Combinatory Categorial Grammar. *Research on Language and Computation*, 4(1):39–75.

Exciting and interesting: issues in the generation of binomials

Ann Copestake
Computer Laboratory,
University of Cambridge,
15 JJ Thomson Avenue,
Cambridge, CB3 0FD, UK
ann.copestake@cl.cam.ac.uk

Aurélie Herbelot
Institut für Linguistik,
Universität Potsdam,
Karl-Liebknecht-Straße 24-25
D-14476 Golm, Germany
herbelot@uni-potsdam.de

Abstract

We discuss the preferred ordering of elements of binomials (e.g., conjunctions such as *fish and chips*, *lager and lime*, *exciting and interesting*) and provide a detailed critique of Benor and Levy's probabilistic account of English binomials. In particular, we discuss the extent to which their approach is suitable as a model of language generation. We describe resources we have developed for the investigation of binomials using a combination of parsed corpora and very large unparsed corpora. We discuss the use of these resources in developing models of binomial ordering, concentrating in particular on the evaluation issues which arise.

1 Introduction

Phrases such as *exciting and interesting* and *gin and tonic* (referred to in the linguistics literature as **binomials**) are generally described as having a semantics which makes the ordering of the conjuncts irrelevant. For instance, *exciting and interesting* might correspond to exciting$'(x) \wedge$ interesting$'(x)$ which is identical in meaning to interesting$'(x) \wedge$exciting$'(x)$. However, in many cases, the binomial is realized with a preferred ordering, and in some cases this preference is so strong that the reverse is perceived as highly marked and may even be difficult to understand. For example, *tonic and gin* has a corpus frequency which is a very small fraction of that of *gin and tonic*. Such cases are referred to as **irreversible binomials**, although the term is sometimes used only for the fully lexicalised, non-compositional examples, such as *odds and ends*.

Of course, realization techniques that utilize very large corpora to decide on word ordering will tend to get the correct ordering for such phrases if they have been seen sufficiently frequently in the training data. But the phenomenon is nevertheless of some practical interest because rare and newly-coined phrases can still demonstrate a strong ordering preference. For instance, the ordering found in the names of mixed drinks, where the alcoholic component comes first, applies not just to the conventional examples such as *gin and tonic*, but also to *brandy and coke*, *lager and lime*, *sake and grapefruit* and (hopefully) unseen combinations such as *armagnac and blackcurrant*.[1] A second issue is that data from an unparsed corpus can be misleading in deciding on binomial order. Furthermore, our own interest is predominantly in developing plausible computational models of human language generation, and from this perspective, using data from extremely large corpora to train a model is unrealistic. Binomials are a particularly interesting construction to look at because they raise two important questions: (1) to what extent does lexicalisation/establishment of phrases play a role in determining order? and (2) is a detailed lexical semantic classification required to accurately predict order?

As far as we are aware, the problem of developing a model of binomial ordering for language generation has not previously been addressed. However, Benor and Levy (2006) have published an important and detailed paper on binomial ordering which we draw on extensively in this work. Their research has the objective of determining how the various constraints which have been proposed in the linguistic literature might interact to determine bino-

[1] One of our reviewers very helpfully consulted a bartender about this generalization, and reports the hypothesis that the alcohol always comes first because it is poured first. However, there is the counter-example *gin and bitters* (another name for pink gin), where the bitters are added first (unless the drink is made in a cocktail shaker, in which case ordering is irrelevant).

mial ordering as observed in a corpus. We present a critical evaluation of that work here, in terms of the somewhat different requirements for a model for language generation.

The issues that we concentrate on in this paper are necessary preliminaries to constructing corpus-based models of binomial reversibility and ordering. These are:

1. Building a suitable corpus of binomials.

2. Developing a corpus-based technique for evaluation.

3. Constructing an initial model to test the evaluation methodology.

In §2, we provide a brief overview of some of the factors affecting binomial ordering and discuss Benor and Levy's work in particular. §3 discusses evaluation issues and motivates some of the decisions we made in deciding on the resources we have developed, described in §4. §5 illustrates the evaluation of a simple model of binomial ordering.

2 Benor and Levy's account

We do not have space here for a proper discussion of the extensive literature on binomials, or indeed for a full discussion of Benor and Levy's paper (henceforth B+L) but instead summarise the aspects which are most important for the current work.

For convenience, we follow B+L in referring to the elements of an ordered binomial as A and B. They only consider binomials of the form 'A and B' where A and B are of the same syntactic category. Personal proper names were excluded from their analysis. Because they required tagged data, they used a combination of Switchboard, Brown and the Wall Street Journal portion of the Penn Treebank to extract binomials, selecting 411 binomial types and all of the corresponding tokens (692 instances).

B+L investigate a considerable number of constraints on binomial ordering which have been discussed in the linguistics literature. They group the features they use into 4 classes: semantic, word frequency, metrical and non-metrical phonological. We will not discuss the last class here, since they found little evidence that it was relevant once the other features were taken into account. The metrical constraints were **lapse** (2 consecutive weak syllables are generally avoided), **length** (A should not have more syllables than B) and **stress** (B should not have ultimate (primary) stress: this feature was actually found to overlap almost entirely with lapse and length). The frequency constraint is that B should not be more frequent than A, based on corpus specific counts of frequency (unsurprisingly, frequency correlates with the length feature).

The semantic constraints are less straightforward since the linguistics literature has discussed many constraints and a variety of possible generalisations. B+L use:

Markedness Divided into **Relative formal**, which includes cases like *flowers and roses* (more general term first) among others and **Perception-based**, which is determined by extra-linguistic knowledge, including cases like *see and hear* (seeing is more salient). B should not be less marked than A. Unfortunately markedness is too complex to summarise adequately here. It is clear that it overlaps with other constraints in some cases, including frequency, since unmarked terms tend to be more frequent.

Iconicity Sequence ordering of events, numbered entities and so on (e.g., *shot and killed*, *eighth and ninth*). If there is such a sequence, the binomial ordering should mirror it.

Power Power includes gender relationships (discussed below), hierarchical relationships (e.g., *clergymen and parishioners*), the 'condiment rule' (e.g., *fish and chips*) and so on. B should not be more powerful than A.

Set Open Construction This is used for certain conventional cases where a given A may occur with multiple Bs: e.g., *nice and*.

Pragmatic A miscellaneous context-dependent constraint, used, for instance, where the binomial ordering mirrors the ordering of other words in the sentence.

B+L looked at the binomials in sentential context to assign the semantic constraints. The iconicity constraint, in particular, is context-dependent. For example, although the sequence *ninth and eighth* looks as though it violates iconicity, we found that a Google search reveals a substantial number of instances, many of which refer to the ninth and eighth centuries BC. In this case, iconicity is actually observed, if we assume that temporal ordering determines the constraint, rather than the ordering of the ordinals.

The aspect of binomials which has received most attention in the literature is the effect of gender: words which refer to (human) males tend to precede those referring to females. For instance (with Google 3-gram percentages for binomials with the masculine term first): *men and women* (85%), *boys and girls* (80%), *male and female* (91%) (exceptions are *father and mother* (51%) and *mothers and fathers* (33%)). There is also an observed bias towards predominantly male names preceding female names. B+L, following previous authors, take gender as an example of the Power feature. For reasons of space we can only touch on this issue very superficially, but it illustrates a distinction between semantic features which we think important. Iconicity generally refers to a sequence of real world events or entities occuring in a particular order, hence its context-dependence. For verbs, at least, there is a truth conditional effect of the ordering of the binomial: *shot and killed* does not mean the same thing as *killed and shot*. Power, on the other hand, is supposed to be about a conventional relationship between the entities. Even if we are currently more interested in chips rather than fish or biscuits rather than tea, we will still tend to refer to *fish and chips* and *tea and biscuits*. The actual ordering may depend on culture,[2] but the assumption is that, within a particular community, the power relationship which the binomial ordering depends on is fixed.

B+L analyse the effects of all the features in detail, and look at a range of models for combining features, with logistic regression being the most successful. This predicts the ordering of 79.2% of the binomial tokens and 76.7% of the types. When semantic constraints apply, they tend to outrank the metrical constraints. B+L found that iconicity, in particular, is a very strong predictor of binomial order.

B+L's stated assumption is that a speaker/writer knows they want to generate a binomial with the words A and B and decides on the order based on the words and the context. It is this order that they are trying to predict. Of course, it is clear that some binomials are non-compositional multiword expressions (e.g., *odds and ends*) which are listed in conventional dictionaries. These can be thought of as 'words with spaces' and, we would argue that the speaker does not have a choice of ordering in such cases. B+L argue that using a model which listed the fixed phrases would be valid in the prediction of binomial tokens, but not binomial types. We do not think this holds in general and return to the issue in §3.

B+L's work is important in being the first account which examines the effect of the postulated constraints in combination. However, from our perspective (which is of course quite different from theirs), there are a number of potential problems. The first is data sparsity: the vast majority of binomial types in their data occur only once. It is impossible to know whether both orderings are frequent for most types. Furthermore, the number of binomial types is rather small for full investigation of semantic features: e.g., Power is marked on only 26 types. The second issue is that the combined models which B+L examine are, in effect, partially trained on the test data, in that the relative contribution of the various factors is optimized on the test data itself. Thirdly, the semantic factors which B+L consider have no independent verification: they were assigned by the authors for the binomials under consideration, a methodology which makes it impossible to avoid the possibility of bias. There was some control over this, in that it was done independently by the two authors with subsequent discussion to resolve disagreements. However, we think that it would be hard to avoid the possibility of bias in the 'Set open' and 'Pragmatic' constraints in particular. Some of the choices seem unintuitive: e.g., we are unsure why there is a Power annotation on *broccoli and cauliflower*, and why *go and vote* would be marked for Iconicity while *went and voted* is not. It seems to us that the definition of some of these semantic factors in the literature (markedness and power in particular) is suf-

[2]Our favourite example is an English-French parallel text where the order of *Queen Elizabeth and President Mitterand* is reversed in the French.

ficiently unclear for reproducible annotation of the type now expected in computational linguistics to be extremely difficult.

Both for practical and theoretical reasons, we are interested in investigating alternative models which rely on a corpus instead of explicit semantic features. Native speakers are aware of some lexicalised and established binomials (see (Sag et al, 2002) for a discussion of lexicalisation vs establishment in multiword expressions), and will tend to generate them in the familiar order. Instead of explicit features being learned for the unseen cases, we want to investigate the possible role of analogy to the known binomials. For instance, if *tea and biscuits* is known, *coffee and cake* might be generated in that ordering by semantic analogy. The work presented in this paper is essentially preparatory to such experiments, although we will discuss an extremely simple corpus-based model in §5.

3 Evaluating models of binomial ordering

In this section, we discuss what models of binomial ordering should predict and how we might evaluate those predictions.

The first question is to decide precisely what we are attempting to model. B+L take the position that the speaker/writer has in mind the two words of the binomial and chooses to generate them in one order or other in a particular context, but this seems problematic for the irreversible binomials and, in any case, is not directly testable. Alternatively we can ask: Given a corpus of sentences where the binomials have been replaced with unordered pairs of AB, can we generate the ordering actually found? Both of these are essentially token-based evaluations, although we could additionally count binomial types, as B+L do.

One problem with these formulations is that, to do them justice, our models would really have to incorporate features from the surrounding context. Factors such as postmodification of the binomial affect the ordering. This type of evaluation would clearly be the right one if we had a model of binomials incorporated into a general realisation model, but it is not clear it is suitable for looking at binomials in isolation.

Perhaps more importantly, to model the irreversible or semi-irreversible binomials, we should take into account the order and degree of reversibility of particular binomial types. It seems problematic to formulate the generation of a lexicalised binomial, such as *odds and ends*, as a process of deciding on the order of the components, since the speaker must have the term in mind as a unit. In terms of the corpus formulation, given the pair AB, the first question in deciding how to realise the phrase is whether the order is actually fixed. The case of established but compositional binomials, such as *fish and chips*, is slightly less clear, but there still seem good grounds for regarding it as a unit (Cruse, 1986). Furthermore, in evaluating a token-based realisation model, we should not penalise the wrong ordering of a reversible binomial as severely as if the binomial were irreversible. From these perspectives, developing a model of ordering of binomial types should be a preliminary to developing a model of binomial tokens. Context would be important in properly modelling the iconicity effect, but is less of an issue for the other ordering constraints. And even though iconicity is context-dependent, there is a very strongly preferred ordering for many of the binomial types where iconicity is relevant.

Thus we argue that it is appropriate to look at the question: Given two words A, B which can be conjoined, what order do we find most frequently in a corpus? Or, in order to look at degree of reversibility: What proportion of the two orderings do we find in a corpus? This means that we require relatively large corpora to obtain good estimates in order to evaluate a model.

Of course, if we are interested in analogical models of binomial ordering, as mentioned at the end of §2, we need a reasonably large corpus of binomials to develop the model. Ideally this should be a different corpus from the one used for evaluation. We note that some experiments on premodifier ordering have found a considerable drop in performance when testing on a different domain (Shaw and Hatzivassiloglou, 1999). Using a single corpus split into training and test data would, of course, be problematic when working with binomial types. We have thus developed a relatively novel methodology of using an automatically parsed corpus in combination with frequencies from Web data. This is discussed in the next section.

4 Binomial corpora and corpus investigation

In this section, we describe the resources we have developed for investigating binomials and addressing some of the evaluation questions introduced in the previous section. We then present an initial analysis of some of the corpus data.

4.1 Benor and Levy data

The appendix of B+L's paper[3] contains a list of the binomials they looked at, plus some of their markup. Although the size of the B+L dataset is too small for many purposes, we found it useful to consider it as a clean source of binomial types for our initial corpus investigation and evaluation. We produced a version of this list excluding the 10 capitalised examples: some of these seem to arise from sentence initial capitals while others are proper names which we decided to exclude from this study. We produced a manually lemmatised version of the list, which results in a slightly reduced number of binomial types: e.g., *bought and sold* and *buy and sell* correspond to a single type. The issue of lemmatisation is slightly problematic in that a few examples are lexicalised with particular inflections, such as *been and gone*. However, our use of parsed data meant that we had to use lemmatization decisions which were compatible with the parser.

4.2 Wikipedia and the Google n-gram corpus

In line with B+L, we assume that binomials are made of two conjuncts with the same part of speech. It is not possible to use an unparsed corpus to extract such constructions automatically: first, the raw text surrounding a conjunction may not correspond to the actual elements of the coordination (e.g., the trigram *dictionary and phrase* in *She bought a dictionary and phrase book*); second, the part of speech information is not available. Using a parsed corpus, however, has disadvantages: in particular, it limits the amount of data available and, consequently, the number of times that a given type can be observed. In this section, we discuss the use of Wikipedia, which is small enough for parsing to be tractable but which turns out to have a fairly representative distribution of binomials. The latter point is demonstrated by comparison with a large dataset: the Google n-gram corpus (Brants and Franz, 2006). Although the Google data is not suitable for the actual task of extracting binomials, because it is not parsed, we hypothesize it is usable to predict the preferred order of a given binomial and to estimate the extent to which it is reversible.

In order to build a corpus of binomials, we process the parsed Wikipedia dump produced by Kummerfeld et al (2010). The parse consists of grammatical relations of the following form:

$$(gr\ word_1\_x\ word_2\_y\ ...\ word_n\_z)$$

where gr is the name of the grammatical relation, $word_{1...n}$ are the arguments of the relation, and $x, y...z$ are the positions of the arguments in the sentence. The lemmatised forms of the arguments, as well as their part of speech, are available separately.

We used the first one million *and* coordinations in the corpus in these experiments. The conjuncts are required to have the same part of speech and to directly precede and follow the coordination. The latter requirement ensures that we retrieve true binomials (phrases, as opposed to distant coordinates). For each binomial in this data, we record a frequency and whether it is found in the reverse order in the same dataset. The frequency of the reverse ordering is similarly collected. Since we intend to compare the Wikipedia data to a larger, unparsed corpus, we merge the counts of all possible parts of speech for a given type in a given ordering, so the counts for *European and American* as nouns and as adjectives, for instance, are added together. We also record the preferred ordering (the one with the highest frequency) of the binomial and the ratio of the frequencies as an indication of (ir)reversibility. In line with our treatment of the B+L data, we disregarded the binomials that coordinate proper names, but noted that a large proportion of proper names found in the Wikipedia data cannot be found in the Google data.[4] The Google corpus also splits (most) hyphen-

[3] http://idiom.ucsd.edu/~rlevy/papers/binomials-sem-alpha-formatted

[4] This suggests that the Google n-gram corpus does not contain much (if any) of the Wikipedia data: the particular dump of Wikipedia from which the parsed data is extracted being in any case several years later than the date that the Google n-gram corpus was produced.

ated words. Since hyphenation is notoriously irregular in English, we disregarded all binomials containing hyphenated words. The resulting data contains 279136 unique binomial types. Around 7600 of those types have a frequency of 10 or more in our Wikipedia subset. As expected, this leaves a large amount of data with low frequency.

We then attempt to verify how close the sparse Wikipedia data is to the Google 3-gram corpus. For each binomial obtained from Wikipedia, we retrieve the frequency of both its orderings in the Google data and, as before, calculate the ratio of the frequencies in the larger corpus. The procedure involves converting the lemmatised forms in the Wikipedia parse back into surface forms. Rather than using a morphological generator, which would introduce noise in our data, we search for the surface forms as they appeared in the original Wikipedia data, as well as for the coordinated base forms (this ensures high recall in cases where the original frequency is low). So for example, given the one instance of the binomial 'sadden and anger' in Wikipedia, appearing as *Saddened and angered* in the corpus, we search for *Saddened and angered*, *sadden and anger* and *anger and sadden*.

Around 30% of the Wikipedia binomials are not in the Google data. We manually spot checked a number of those and confirmed that they were unavailable from the Google data, regardless of inflection. Examples of binomials not found in the n-gram corpus include *dagger and saber*, *sagacious and firm* and (rather surprisingly) *gay and flamboyant*. 19% of the Wikipedia binomials have a different preferred order in the Google corpus. As expected, most of those have a low frequency in Wikipedia. For the binomials with an occurrence count over 40, the agreement on ordering is high (around 96%). Furthermore, many of those disagreements are not 'real' in that they concern binomials found with a high dispreferred to preferred order ratio. Disregarding cases where this ratio is over 0.3 lowers the initial disagreement figure to 7%. We will argue in §4.4 that true irreversibility can be shown to roughly correspond to a ratio of 0.1. At this cutoff, the percentage of disagreements between the two corpora is only 2%. Thus we found no evidence that the encyclopaedic nature of Wikipedia has a significant skewing effect on the frequencies. We thus believe that Wikipedia is a suitable dataset for training an automatic binomial ordering system.

4.3 Lexicalisation

Our basic methodology for investigation of lexicalisation was to check online dictionaries for the phrases. However, deciding whether a binomial should be regarded as a fixed phrase is not entirely straightforward. For instance, consider *warm and fuzzy*. At first sight, it might appear compositional, but the particular use of *fuzzy*, referring to feelings, is not the usual one. While *warm and fuzzy* is not listed in most dictionaries we have examined, it has an entry in the *Urban Dictionary*[5] and is used in examples illustrating that particular usage of *fuzzy* in the online Merriam-Webster.[6] Another case from the B+L data is *nice and toasty*, which again is used in a Merriam-Webster example.[7]

We therefore used a manual search procedure to check for lexicalisation of the B+L binomials. We used a broad notion of lexicalisation, treating a phrase as lexicalised if it occurred as an entry in one or more online English dictionaries using Google search. We included a few phrases as semi-lexicalised when they were given in examples in dictionaries produced by professional lexicographers, but this was, to some extent, a subjective decision. Since such a search is time-consuming, we only checked examples which one of us (a native British English speaker) intuitively considered might be lexicalised. We first validated that this would not cause too great a loss of recall by checking a small subset of the B+L data exhaustively: this did not reveal any additional examples.

Using these criteria, we found 39 lexicalised binomial types in the B+L data, of which 7 were semi-lexicalised.[8] The phrases *backwards and forwards*, *backward and forward*, *day and night*, *salt and pepper* and *in and out* are lexicalised (or semi-lexicalised) in both orders.

[5] `http://www.urbandictionary.com/`

[6] `http://www.merriam-webster.com/`

[7] The convention of indicating semi-fixed phrases in examples is quite common in lexicography, especially in dictionaries intended for language learners.

[8] There are 40 tokens, because *cut and dry* and *cut and dried* are both lexicalised. An additional example, *foot-loose and fancy-free*, might be included, but we did not find it in any dictionary with that hyphenation.

4.4 Reversibility and corpus evidence

There are a number of possible reasons why a particular binomial type AB might (almost) always appear in one ordering (*A and B* or *B and A*):

1. The phrase *A and B* (*B and A*) might be fully lexicalised (word with spaces).

2. The binomial might have a compositional meaning, but have a conventional ordering. A particular binomial AB might be established with that ordering (e.g., *gin and tonic* is established for most British and American speakers) or might belong to a conventional pattern (e.g., *armagnac and blackcurrant*, *sole and artichokes*).

3. The binomial could refer to a sequence of real world events or entities which almost invariably occur in a particular order. For example, *shot and killed* has a frequency of 241675 in the Google 3-gram corpus, as opposed to 158 for *killed and shot*. This ratio is larger that that of many of the lexicalised binomials.

Relatively few of the binomials from the B+L data are completely irreversible according to the Google 3-gram data. There are instances of the reverse of even obviously fixed phrases, such as *odds and ends*. Of course, there is no available context in the 3-gram data, but we investigated some of these cases by online search for the reversed phrases. This indicates a variety of sources of noise, including wordplay (e.g., Beckett's play *Ends and Odds*), different word senses (e.g., *toasty and nice* occurs when *toasty* is used to describe wine) and false positives from hyphenated words etc.

We can obtain a crude estimate of extent to which binomials which should be irreversible actually turn up in the 'wrong' order by looking at the clearly lexicalised phrases discussed in §4.3. Excluding the cases where both orders are lexicalised, the mean proportion of inverted cases is about 3%. There are a few outliers, such as *there and back* and *now and then* which have more than 10% inverted: however, these all involve very frequent closed class words which are more likely to show up in spurious contexts. We therefore tentatively conclude that up to 10% of the tokens of a open-class irreversible binomial could be inverted in the 3-gram corpus, but that we can take higher ratios as evidence for a degree of genuine reversibility.

5 An initial model

We developed an initial n-gram-based model for ordering using the Wikipedia-derived counts. The approach is very similar to that presented in (Malouf, 2000) for adjective ordering. We use the observed order of binomials where possible and back off to counts of a lexeme's position as first or second conjunct over all binomials (i.e., we use what Malouf refers to as **positional probabilities**).

To be more precise, assume that the task is to predict the order $a \prec b$ or $b \prec a$ for a given lexeme pair a,b. We use the notation $C(\text{a and b})$ and $C(\text{b and a})$ to refer to the counts in a given corpus of the two orderings of the binomial (i.e., we count all inflections of a and b). $C(\text{a and})$ refers to the count of all binomials with the lexeme a as the first conjunct, $C(\text{and a})$ all binomials with a as the second conjunct, and so on. We predict $a \prec b$

$$\begin{array}{ll} \text{if} & C(\text{a and b}) > C(\text{b and a}) \\ \text{or} & C(\text{a and b}) = C(\text{a and b}) \\ & \quad \text{and} \\ & C(\text{a and})C(\text{and b}) > C(\text{b and})C(\text{and a}) \end{array}$$

and conversely for $b \prec a$. Most of the cases where the condition $C(\text{a and b}) = C(\text{a and b})$ is true occur when $C(\text{a and b}) = C(\text{a and b}) = 0$ but we also use the positional probabilities to break ties in the counts. We could, of course, define this in terms of probability estimates and investigate various forms of smoothing and interpolation, but for our initial purposes it is adequate to see how this very simple model behaves.

We obtained counts for the model from the Wikipedia-derived data and evaluated it on the binomial types derived from B+L (as described in §4.1). There were only 9 cases where there was no prediction, so for the sake of simplicity, we default to alphabetic ordering in those cases. In Table 1, we show the results evaluating against the B+L majority decision and against the Google 3-gram majority. Because not all the B+L binomials are found in the Google data, the numbers of binomial types evaluated against the Google data is slightly lower. In addition to the overall figures, we also show the relative accuracy of the bigram prediction vs the backoff and the different accuracies on the lexicalised and non-lexicalised data. In Table 2, we group the results according to the ratio of the less frequent order in the Google data and by frequency.

Unsurprisingly, performance on more frequent binomials and lexicalised binomials is better and the bigram performance, where available, is better than the backoff to positional probabilities. The scores when evaluated on the Google corpus are generally higher than those on the B+L counts, as expected given the noise created by the data sparsity in B+L combined with the effect of frequency.

One outcome from our experiments is that it does not seem essential to treat the lexicalised examples separately from the high frequency, low reversibility cases. Since determining lexicalisation is time-consuming and error-prone, this is a useful result.

The model described does not predict whether or not a given binomial is irreversible, but our analysis of the data strongly suggests that this would be important in developing more realistic models. An obvious extension would be to generate probability estimates of orderings and to compare these with the observed Google 3-gram data.

Although n-gram models are completely standard in computational linguistics, their applicability to modelling human performance on a task is not straightforward. Minimally, if we were to propose that humans were using such a model as part of their decision on binomial ordering, it would be necessary to demonstrate that the counts we are relying on correspond to data which it is plausible to assume that a human could have been exposed to. This is not a trivial consideration. We would, of course, expect to obtain higher scores on this task by using counts derived from the Google n-gram corpus rather than from Wikipedia, but this would be completely unrealistic from a psycholinguistic perspective. We should emphasize, therefore, that the model presented here is simply intended as an initial exercise in developing distributional models of binomial ordering, which allows us to check whether the resources we have developed might be an adequate basis for more serious modelling and whether the evaluation schemes are reasonable.

6 Conclusion

We have demonstrated that we can make use of a combination of corpora to build resources for development and evaluation of models of binomial ordering.[9] One novel aspect is our use of an automatically parsed corpus, another is the use of combined corpora. If binomial ordering is primarily determined by universal linguistic factors, we would not expect the relative frequency to differ very substantially between large corpora. The cases where we did observe differences in preferred ordering between the Wikipedia and Google data are predominantly ones where the Wikipedia frequency is low or the binomial is highly reversible. We have investigated several properties of binomials using this data and produced a simple initial model. We tested this on the relatively small number of binomials used by Benor and Levy (2006), but in future work we will evaluate on a much larger subset of our corpus. Our intention is to develop further models which use analogy (morphological and distributional semantic similarity) to known binomials to predict degree of reversibility and ordering. This will allow us to investigate whether human performance can be modelled without the use of explicit semantic features.

We briefly touched on Malouf's (2000) work on prenominal adjective ordering in our discussion of the initial model. There are some similarities between these tasks, and in fact adjectives in binomials tend to occur in the same order when they appear as prenominal adjectives (e.g., *cold and wet* and *cold wet* are preferred over the inverse orders). However, the binomial problem is considerably more complex. Binomials are much more variable because they involve all the main syntactic categories. Furthermore, adjective ordering is considerably easier to investigate because an unparsed corpus can be used, the semantic features which have been postulated are more straightforward than for binomials and lexicalisation of adjective sequences is not an issue. We hypothesize that it should be possible to develop similar analogical models for adjective ordering and binomials which could be relevant for other constructions where ordering is only partially determined by syntax. In the long term, we would like to in-

[9] Available from `http://www.cl.cam.ac.uk/research/nl/nl-download/binomials/`

	n B+L	n Google	accuracy B+L (%)	accuracy Google (%)
Overall	380	305	69	79
Bigram	187	185	79	89
Pos Prob	184	117	61	65
Unknown	9	3	33	0
Lexicalised	34	34	87	94
Non-lexicalised	346	271	67	77

Table 1: Evaluation of initial model, showing effects of lexicalisation. (n B+L and n Google indicates the number of binomial types evaluated)

		n	accuracy B+L (%)	accuracy Google (%)
Google count	0	75	59	-
	1–1000	71	56	68
	1001–10000	81	70	67
	> 10000	153	80	91
Google ratio	0	11	64	64
	0–0.1	41	94	93
	0.1–0.25	33	75	85
	> 0.25	220	68	76

Table 2: Evaluation of initial model, showing effects of frequency and reversibility.

vestigate using such models in conjunction with a grammar-based realizer (cf (Velldal, 2007), (Cahill and Riester, 2009)). However, for an initial investigation of the role of semantics and lexicalisation, looking at the binomial construction in isolation is more tractable.

Acknowledgments

This work was partially supported by a fellowship to Aurélie Herbelot from the Alexander von Humboldt Foundation. We are grateful to the reviewers for their comments.

References

Sarah Benor and Roger Levy. 2006. *The Chicken or the Egg? A Probabilistic Analysis of English Binomials.* Language, **82** 233–78.

Thorsten Brants and Alex Franz. 2006. *The Google Web 1T 5-gram Corpus Version 1.1.* LDC2006T13.

Aoife Cahill and Arndt Riester. 2009. *Incorporating Information Status into Generation Ranking.* In Proceedings of the 47th Annual Meeting of the ACL, pp. 817-825, Suntec, Singapore. Association for Computational Linguistics.

D. Alan Cruse. 1986. Lexical Semantics. Cambridge University Press.

Jonathan K. Kummerfeld, Jessika Rosener, Tim Dawborn, James Haggerty, James R. Curran, Stephen Clark. 2010. *Faster parsing by supertagger adaptation* Proceedings of the 48th Annual Meeting of the Association for Computational Linguistics, Uppsala, Sweden, pages 345–355

Rob Malouf. 2000. The order of prenominal adjectives in natural language generation. In Proceedings of the 38th Annual Meeting of the Association for Computational Linguistics (ACL 2000), Hong Kong.

Ivan Sag, Tim Baldwin, Francis Bond, Ann Copestake, and Dan Flickinger. 2002. *Multiword expressions: A pain in the neck for NLP.* In Third International Conference on Intelligent Text Processing and Computational Linguistics (CICLING 2002), pages 1–15, Mexico City, Mexico.

James Shaw and Vasileios Hatzivassiloglou. 1999. *Ordering among premodifiers.* In Proceedings of the 37th Annual Meeting of the Association for Computational Linguistics, pages 135–143, College Park, Maryland.

Eric Velldal. 2007. *Empirical Realization Ranking.* Ph.D. thesis, University of Oslo, Department of Informatics.

Discriminative features in reversible stochastic attribute-value grammars

Daniël de Kok
University of Groningen
d.j.a.de.kok@rug.nl

Abstract

Reversible stochastic attribute-value grammars (de Kok et al., 2011) use one model for parse disambiguation and fluency ranking. Such a model encodes preferences with respect to syntax, fluency, and appropriateness of logical forms, as weighted features. Reversible models are built on the premise that syntactic preferences are shared between parse disambiguation and fluency ranking.

Given that reversible models also use features that are specific to parsing or generation, there is the possibility that the model is trained to rely on these directional features. If this is true, the premise that preferences are shared between parse disambiguation and fluency ranking does not hold.

In this work, we compare and apply feature selection techniques to extract the most discriminative features from directional and reversible models. We then analyse the contributions of different classes of features, and show that reversible models do rely on task-independent features.

1 Introduction

Reversible stochastic attribute-value grammars (de Kok et al., 2011) provide an elegant framework that fully integrates parsing and generation. The most important contribution of this framework is that it uses one conditional maximum entropy model for fluency ranking and parse disambiguation. In such a model, the probability of a derivation d is conditioned on a set of input constraints c that restrict the set of derivations allowed by a grammar to those corresponding to a particular sentence (parsing) or logical form (generation):

$$p(d|c) = \frac{1}{Z(c)} exp \sum_i w_i f_i(c,d) \quad (1)$$

$$Z(c) = \sum_{d' \in \Omega(c)} exp \sum_i w_i f_i(c,d') \quad (2)$$

Here, $\Omega(c)$ is the set of derivations for input c, $f_i(c,d)$ the value of feature f_i in derivation d of c, and w_i is the weight of f_i. Reversibility is operationalized during training by imposing a constraint on a given feature f_i with respect to the sentences T in the parse disambiguation treebank and logical forms L in the fluency ranking treebank. This constraint is:

$$\sum_{c \in C} \sum_{d \in \Omega(c)} \tilde{p}(c) p(d|c) f_i(c,d) - \tilde{p}(c,d) f_i(c,d) = 0 \quad (3)$$

Where $C = T \cup L$, $\tilde{p}(c)$ is the empirical probability of a set of constraints c, and $\tilde{p}(c,d)$ the joint probability of a set of constraints c and a derivation d.

Reversible stochastic-attribute grammars rest on the premise that preferences are shared between language comprehension and production. For instance, in Dutch, subject fronting is preferred over direct object fronting. If models for parse disambiguation and fluency ranking do not share preferences with respect to fronting, it would be difficult for a parser to recover the logical form that was the input to a generator.

Reversible models incorporate features that are specific to parse disambiguation and fluency ranking, as well as features that are used for both tasks. Previous work (Cahill et al., 2007; de Kok, 2010) has shown through feature analysis that task-independent features are indeed useful in directional models. However, since reversible models assign just one weight to each feature regardless the task, one particular concern is that much of their discriminatory power is provided by task-specific features. If this is true, the premise that similar preferences are used in parsing and generation does not hold.

In this work, we will isolate the most discriminative features of reversible models through feature selection, and make a quantitative and qualitative analysis of these features. Our aim is to to verify that reversible models do rely on features used both in parsing and generation.

To find the most effective features of a model, we need an effective feature selection method. Section 2 describes three such methods: *grafting*, *grafting-light*, and *gain-informed selection*. These methods are compared empirically in Section 4 using the experimental setup described in Section 3. We then use the best feature selection method to perform quantitative and qualitative analyses of reversible models in Sections 5 and 6.

2 Feature selection

Feature selection is a procedure that attempts to extract a subset of discriminative features $S \subset F$ from a set of features F, such that a model using S performs comparable to a model using F and $|S| \ll |F|$.

As discussed in De Kok (2010), a good feature selection method should handle three kinds of redundancies in feature sets: features that rarely change value; features that overlap; and noisy features. Also, for a qualitative evaluation of fluency ranking, it is necessary to have a ranking of features by discriminative power.

De Kok (2010) compares frequency-based selection, correlation selection, and a gain-informed selection method. In that work, it was found that the gain-informed selection method outperforms frequency-based and correlation selection. For this reason we exclude the latter two methods from our experiments. Other commonly used selection methods for maximum entropy models include ℓ_1 regularization (Tibshirani, 1996), grafting (Perkins et al., 2003; Riezler and Vasserman, 2004), and grafting-light (Zhu et al., 2010). In the following sections, we will give a description of these selection methods.

2.1 $\ell 1$ regularization

During the training of maximum entropy models, regularization is often applied to avoid unconstrained feature weights and overfitting. If $L(w)$ is the objective function that is minimized during training, a regularizer $\Omega_q(w)$ is added as a penalty for extreme weights (Tibshirani, 1996):

$$C(w) = L(w) + \Omega_q(w) \tag{4}$$

Given that the maximum entropy training procedure attempts to minimize the negative log-likelihood of the model, the penalized objective function is:

$$C(w) = -\sum_{c,d} \tilde{p}(c,d) log(p(d|c)) + \Omega_q(w) \tag{5}$$

The regularizer has the following form:

$$\Omega_q(w) = \lambda \sum_{i=1}^{n} |w_i|^q$$

Setting $q = 1$ in the regularizer function gives a so-called ℓ_1 regularizer and amounts to applying a double-exponential prior distribution with $\mu = 0$. Since the double-exponential puts much of its probability mass near its mean, the ℓ_1 regularizer has a tendency to force weights towards zero, providing integral feature selection and avoiding unbounded weights. Increasing λ strengthens the regularizer, and forces more feature weights to be zero.

Given an appropriate value for λ, ℓ_1 regularization can exclude features that change value infrequently, as well as noisy features. However, it does not guarantee to exclude overlapping features, since the weight mass can be distributed among overlapping features. ℓ_1 regularization also does not fulfill a necessary characteristic for the present task, in that it does not provide a ranking based on the discriminative power of features.

2.2 Grafting

Grafting (Perkins et al., 2003) adds incremental feature selection during the training of a maximum entropy model. The selection process is a repetition of two steps: 1. a gradient-based heuristic selects the most promising feature from the set of unselected features Z, adding it to the set of selected features S, and 2. a full optimization of weights is performed over all features in S. These steps are repeated until a stopping condition is triggered.

During the first step, the gradient of each unselected feature $f_i \in Z$ is calculated with respect to the model p_S, that was trained with the set of selected features, S:

$$\left| \frac{\partial L(w_S)}{\partial w_i} \right| = p_S(f_i) - \tilde{p}(f_i) \quad (6)$$

The feature with the largest gradient is removed from Z and added to S.

The stopping condition for grafting integrates the ℓ_1 regularizer in the grafting method. Note that when ℓ_1 regularization is applied, a feature is only included (has a non-zero weight) if its penalty is outweighted by its contribution to the reduction of the objective function. Consequently, only features for which $\left| \frac{\partial L(w_S)}{\partial w_i} \right| > \lambda$ holds are eligible for selection. This is enforced by stopping selection if for all f_i in Z

$$\left| \frac{\partial L(w_S)}{\partial w_i} \right| \leq \lambda \quad (7)$$

Although grafting uses ℓ_1 regularization, its iterative nature avoids selecting overlapping features. For instance, if f_1 and f_2 are identical, and f_1 is added to the model p_S, $\left| \frac{\partial L(w_S)}{\partial w_2} \right|$ will amount to zero.

Performing a full optimization after each selected feature is computationally expensive. Riezler and Vasserman (2004) observe that during the feature step selection a larger number of features can be added to the model (n-best selection) without a loss of accuracy in the resulting model. However, this so-called *n-best grafting* may introduce overlapping features.

2.3 Grafting-light

The grafting-light method (Zhu et al., 2010) operates using the same selection step as grafting, but improves performance over grafting by applying one iteration of gradient-descent during the optimization step rather than performing a full gradient-descent. As such, grafting-light gradually works towards the optimal weights, while grafting always finds the optimal weights for the features in S during each iteration.

Since grafting-light does not perform a full gradient-descent, an additional stopping condition is required, since the model may still not be optimal even though no more features can be selected. This additional condition requires that change in value of the objective function incurred by the last gradient-descent is smaller than a predefined threshold.

2.4 Gain-informed selection

Gain-informed feature selection methods calculate the gain $\Delta L(S, f_i)$ of adding a feature $f_i \in Z$ to the model. If $L(w_S)$ is the negative log-likelihood of p_S, $\Delta L(S, f_i)$ is defined as:

$$\Delta L(S, f_i) \equiv L(w_S) - L(w_{S \cup f_i}) \quad (8)$$

During each selection step, the feature that gives the highest gain is selected. The calculation of $L(p_{S \cup f_i})$ requires a full optimization over the weights of the features in $S \cup f_i$. Since it is computationally intractable to do this for every f_i in Z, Berger et al. (1996) propose to estimate the weight w_i of the candidate feature f_i, while assuming that the weights of features in S stay constant. Under this assumption, w_i can be estimated using a simple line search method.

However, Zhou et al. (2003) observe that, despite this simplification, the gain-informed selection method proposed by Berger et al. (1996) still recalculates the weights of all the candidate features during every cycle. They observe that the gains of candidate features rarely increase. If it is assumed that the gain of adding a feature does indeed never increase as a result of adding another feature, the gains of features during the previous iteration can be kept.

To account for features that become ineffective, the gain of the highest ranked feature is recalculated. The highest ranked feature is selected if it remains the best feature after this recalculation. Otherwise, the same procedure is repeated for the next best feature.

De Kok (2010) modifies the method of Zhou et al. (2003) for ranking tasks. In the present work, we also apply this method, but perform a full optimization of feature weights in p_S every n cycles.

Since this selection method uses the gain of a feature in its selection criterion, it excludes noisy and redundant features. Overlapping features are also excluded since their gain diminishes after selecting one of the overlapping features.

3 Experimental setup and evaluation

3.1 Treebanks

We carry out our experiments using the Alpino dependency parser and generator for Dutch (van Noord, 2006; de Kok and van Noord, 2010). Two newspaper corpora are used in the experiments. The training data consists of the cdbl part of the Eindhoven corpus[1] (7,154 sentences). Syntactic annotations are available from the Alpino Treebank[2] (van der Beek et al., 2002). Part of the Trouw newspaper of 2001 is used for evaluation[3]. Syntactic annotations are part of LASSY[4] (van Noord et al., 2010), part WR-P-P-H (2,267 sentences).

3.2 Features

In our experiments, we use the features described in De Kok et al. (2011). In this section, we provide a short summarization of the types of features that are used.

Word adjacency. Word and Alpino part-of-speech tag trigram models are used as auxiliary distributions (Johnson and Riezler, 2000). In both models, linear interpolation smoothing is applied to handle unknown trigrams, and Laplacian smoothing for unknown unigrams. The trigram models have been trained on the Twente Nieuws Corpus (approximately 100 million words), excluding the Trouw 2001 corpus. In parsing, the value of the word trigram model is constant across derivations of a given input sentence.

Lexical frames. The parser applies lexical analysis to find all possible subcategorization frames for tokens in the input sentence. Since some frames occur more frequently in good parses than others, two feature templates record the use of frames in derivations. An additional feature implements an auxiliary distribution of frames, trained on a large corpus of automatically annotated sentences (436 million words). The values of lexical frame features are constant for all derivations in sentence realization, unless the frame is underspecified in the logical form.

Dependency relations. Several templates describe aspects of the dependency structure. For each dependency relation multiple dependency features are extracted. These features list the dependency relation, and characteristics of the head and dependent, such as their roots or part of speech tags. Additionally, features are used to implement auxiliary distributions for selectional preferences (van Noord, 2007). In generation, the values of these features are constant across derivations corresponding to a given logical form.

Syntactic features. Syntactic features include features that record the application of grammar rules, as well as the application of a rule in the context of another rule. Additionally, there are features describing more complex syntactic patterns, such as fronting of subjects and other noun phrases, orderings in the middle field, long-distance dependencies, and parallelism of conjuncts in coordinations.

3.3 Parse disambiguation

To create training and evaluation data for parse disambiguation, the treebanks described in section 3.1 are parsed, extracting the first 3000 derivations. On average, there are about 649 derivations for the sentences in the training data, and 402 derivations for the sentences in the test data.

Since the parser does not always yield the correct parse, the concept accuracy (CA) (van Noord,

[1] `http://www.inl.nl/corpora/eindhoven-corpus`

[2] `http://www.let.rug.nl/vannoord/trees/`

[3] `http://hmi.ewi.utwente.nl/TwNC`

[4] `http://www.inl.nl/corpora/lassy-corpus`

2006) of each derivation is calculated to estimate its quality. The highest scoring derivations for each input are marked as correct, all other derivations are marked as incorrect. Features are then extracted from each derivation.

The concept accuracy is calculated based on the named dependency relations of the candidate and correct parses. If $D_p(t)$ is the bag of dependencies produced by the parser for sentence t and $D_g(t)$ is the bag of dependencies of the correct (gold-standard) parse, concept accuracy is defined as:

$$\mathrm{CA} = \frac{\sum_{t \in T} |D_p(t) \cap D_g(t)|}{\sum_{t \in T} \max(|D_p(t)|, |D_g(t)|)} \tag{9}$$

The procedure outlined above gives examples of correct and incorrect derivations to train the model, and derivations to test the resulting model.

3.4 Fluency ranking

For training and evaluation of the fluency ranker, we use the same treebanks as in parse disambiguation. We assume that the sentence that corresponds to a dependency structure in the treebank is the correct realization of that dependency structure. We parse each sentence in the treebank, extracting the dependency structure that is the most similar to that in the treebank. We perform this step to assure that it is possible to generate from the given dependency structure. We then use the Alpino chart generator to make all possible derivations and realizations conforming to that dependency structure. Due to a limit on generation time, some longer sentences and corresponding dependency structures are excluded from the data. The average sentence length was 15.7 tokens, with a maximum of 26 tokens.

Since the sentence in the treebank cannot always be produced exactly, we estimate the quality of each realization using the General Text Matcher (GTM) method (Melamed et al., 2003). The best-scoring derivations are marked as correct, the other derivations are marked as incorrect. Finally, features are extracted from these derivations.

The General Text Matcher method marks all corresponding tokens of a candidate realization and the correct realization in a grid, and finds the maximum matching (the largest subset of marks, such that no marks are in the same row or column). The size of the matching M is then determined using the lengths of runs r in the matching (a run is a diagonal of marks), rewarding longer runs:

$$size(M) = \sqrt{\sum_{r \in M} length(r)^2} \tag{10}$$

This method has been shown to have the highest correlation with human judgments in a related language (German), using a comparable system (Cahill, 2009).

3.5 Training

Models are trained by extracting an informative sample of $\Omega(c)$ for each c in the training data (Osborne, 2000). This informative sample consists of at most 100 randomly selected derivations.

We then apply feature selection on the training data. We let each method select 1711 features. This number is derived from the number of non-zero features that training a model with a ℓ_1 norm coefficient of 0.0002 gives. Grafting and grafting-light selection are applied using TinyEst[5]. For gain-informed selection, we use FeatureSqueeze[6]. For all three methods, we add 10 features to the model during each selection step.

3.6 Evaluation

We evaluate each selection method stepwise. We train and evaluate a model on the best-n features according to each selection method, for $n = [0..1711]$. In each case, the feature weights are estimated with TinyEst using a ℓ_1 norm coefficient of 0.0002. This stepwise evaluation allows us to capture the effectiveness of each method.

Parse disambiguation and fluency ranking models are evaluated on the WR-P-P-H corpus that was described in Section 3.1, using CA and GTM scores respectively.

4 Evaluation of feature selection methods

4.1 Incremental feature selection

Figure 1 shows the performance of the feature selection methods for parse disambiguation. This graph shows that that both grafting methods are far more

[5]`http://github.com/danieldk/tinyest`

[6]`https://github.com/rug-compling/featuresqueeze`

effective than gain-informed selection. We can also see that only a small number of features is required to construct a competitive model. Selecting more features improves the model only gradually.

Figure 2 shows the performance of the feature selection methods in fluency ranking. Again, we see the same trend as in parse disambiguation. The grafting and grafting-light methods outperform gain-informed selection, with the grafting method coming out on top. In feature selection, even a smaller number of features is required to train an effective model. After selecting more than approximately 50 features, adding features only improves the model very gradually.

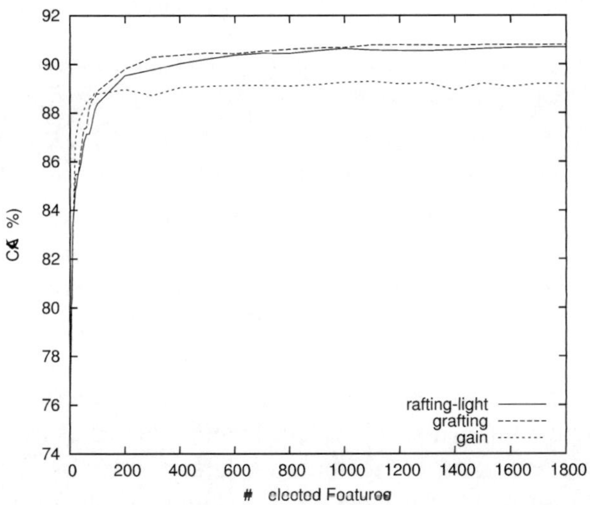

Figure 1: Application of feature selection methods to parse disambiguation

4.2 Selection using an ℓ_1 prior

During our experiments, we also evaluated the effect of using an ℓ_1 prior in Alpino to see if it is worthwile to replace feature selection using a frequency cut-off (Malouf and van Noord, 2004). Using Alpino's default configuration with a frequency cut-off of 2 and an ℓ_2 prior with $\sigma^2 = 1000$ the system had a CA-score of 90.94% using 25237 features. We then trained a model, applying an ℓ_1 prior with a norm coefficient of 0.0002. With this model, the system had a CA-score of 90.90% using 2346 features.

In generation, Alpino uses a model with the same frequency cut-off and ℓ_2 prior. This model has 1734 features features and achieves a GTM score of 0.7187. Applying the ℓ_1 prior reduces the number

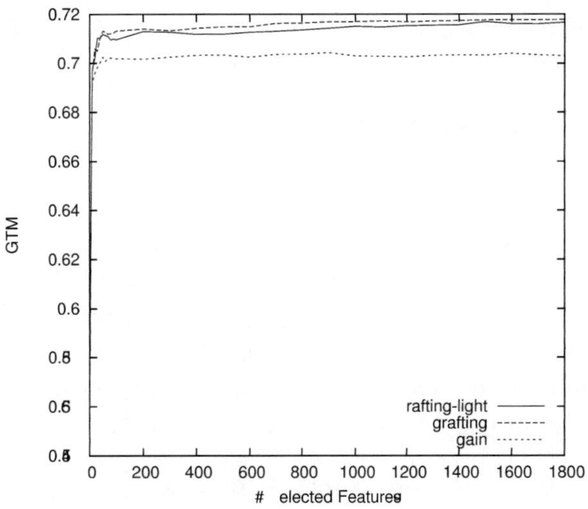

Figure 2: Effectiveness of feature selection methods in fluency ranking. Both grafting methods outperform gain-based ranking

of features to 607, while mildly increasing the GTM score to 0.7188.

These experiments show that the use of ℓ_1 priors can compress models enormously, even compared to frequency-based feature selection, while retaining the same levels of accuracy.

5 Quantitative analysis of reversible models

For a quantitative analysis of highly discriminative features, we extract the 300 most effective features of the fluency ranking, parse disambiguation, and reversible models using grafting. We then divide features into five classes: *dependency* (enumeration of dependency triples), *lexical* (readings of words), *n-gram* (word and tag trigram auxiliary distributions), *rule* (identifiers of grammar rules), and *syntactic* (abstract syntactic features). Of these classes, *rule* and *syntactic* features are active during both parse disambiguation and fluency ranking.

In the quantitative analyses, we train a model for each selection step. The models contain the 1 to 300 best features. Using these models, we can calculate the contribution of feature f_i to the improvement according to some evaluation function e

$$c(f_i) = \frac{e(p_{0..i}) - e(p_{0..i-1})}{e(p_{0..n}) - e(p_0)} \tag{11}$$

where $p_{0..i}$ is a model trained with the i most discriminative features, p_0 is the uniform model, and $n = 300$.

5.1 Parse disambiguation

Table 1 provides class-based counts of the 300 most discriminative features for the parse disambiguation and reversible models. Since the n-gram features are not active during parse disambiguation, they are not selected for the parse disambiguation model. All other classes of features are used in the parse disambiguation model. The reversible model uses all classes of features.

Class	Directional	Reversible
Dependency	93	84
Lexical	24	24
N-gram	0	2
Rule	156	154
Syntactic	27	36

Table 1: Per-class counts of the best 300 features according to the grafting method.

Contributions per feature class in parse disambiguation are shown in table 2. In the directional parse disambiguation model, parsing-specific features (*dependency* and *lexical*) account for 55% of the improvement over the uniform model.

In the reversible model, there is a shift of contribution towards task-independent features. When applying this model, the contribution of parsing-specific features to the improvement over the uniform model is reduced to 45.79%.

We can conclude from the per-class feature contributions in the directional parse disambiguation model and the reversible model, that the reversible model does not put more emphasis on parsing-specific features. Instead, the opposite is true: task-independent features are more important in the reversible model than the directional model.

5.2 Fluency ranking

Table 3 provides class-based counts of the 300 most discriminative features of the fluency ranking and reversible models. During fluency ranking, dependency features and lexical features are not active.

Table 4 shows the per-class contribution to the improvement in accuracy for the directional and reversible models. Since the dependency and lexical

Class	Directional	Reversible
Dependency	21.53	13.35
Lexical	33.68	32.62
N-gram	0.00	0.00
Rule	37.61	47.35
Syntactic	7.04	6.26

Table 2: Per-class contribution to the improvement of the model over the base baseline in parse disambiguation.

Class	Directional	Reversible
Dependency	0	84
Lexical	0	24
N-gram	2	2
Rule	181	154
Syntactic	117	36

Table 3: Per-class counts of the best 300 features according to the grafting method.

features are not active during fluency ranking, it may come as a surprise that their contribution is negative in the reversible model. Since they are used for parse disambiguation, they have an effect on weights of task-independent features. This phenomenon did not occur when using the reversible model for parse disambiguation, because the features specific to fluency ranking (n-gram features) were selected as the most discriminative features in the reversible model. Consequently, the reversible models with one and two features were uniform models from the perspective of parse disambiguation.

Class	Directional	Reversible
Dependency	0.00	-4.21
Lexical	0.00	-1.49
N-gram	81.39	83.41
Rule	14.15	16.45
Syntactic	3.66	4.59

Table 4: Per-class contribution to the improvement of the model over the baseline in fluency ranking.

Since active features compensate for this loss in the reversible model, we cannot directly compare per-class contributions. To this end, we normalize the contribution of all positively contributing features, leading to table 5. Here, we can see that the reversible model does not shift more weight towards task-specific features. On the contrary, there is a mild effect in the opposite direction here as well.

Class	Directional	Reversible
N-gram	81.39	79.89
Rule	14.15	15.75
Syntactic	3.66	4.39

Table 5: Classes giving a net positive distribution, with normalized contributions.

6 Qualitative analysis of reversible models

While the quantitative evaluation shows that task-independent features remain important in reversible models, we also want to get an insight into the actual features that were used. Since it is unfeasible to study the 300 best features in detail, we extract the 20 best features.

Grafting-10 is too course-grained for this task, since it selects the first 10 features solely by their gradients, while there may be overlap in those features. To get the most accurate list possible, we perform grafting-1 selection to extract the 20 most effective features. We show these features in table 6 with their polarities. The polarity indicates whether a feature is an indicator for a good (+) or bad (-) derivation.

We now provide a description of these features by category.

Word/tag trigrams. The most effective features in fluency ranking are the n-gram auxiliary distributions (1, 3). The word n-gram model settles preferences with respect to fixed expressions and common word orders. It also functions as a (probabilistic) filter of archaic inflections and incorrect inflections that are not known to the Alpino lexicon. The tag n-gram model help picking a sequence of part-of-speech tags that is plausible.

Frame selection. Various features assist in the selection of proper subcategorization frames for words. This currently affects parse disambiguation mostly. There is virtually no ambiguity of frames during generation, and a stem/frame combination normally only selects one inflection. The most effective feature for frame selection is (2), which is an auxiliary distribution of words and corresponding frames based on a large automatically annotated

Rank	Polarity	Feature
1	+	ngram_lm
2	+	z_f2
3	+	ngram_tag
4	-	r1(np_n)
5	+	r2(np_det_n,2,n_n_pps)
6	-	p1(pardepth)
7	+	r2(vp_mod_v,3,vproj_vc)
8	-	r2(vp_arg_v(np),2,vproj_vc)
9	-	f1(adj)
10	+	r2(vp_mod_v,2,optpunct(e))
11	-	s1(non_subj_np_topic)
12	+	r1(n_adj_n)
13	+	dep23(prep,hd/pc,verb)
14	+	r1(optpunct(e))
15	+	dep34(van,prep,hd/mod,noun)
16	+	dep23(noun,hd/su,verb)
17	+	p1(par)
18	-	r1(vp_v_mod)
19	+	dep23(prep,hd/mod,verb)
20	-	f1(verb(intransitive))

Table 6: The twenty most discriminative features of the reversible model, and their polarities.

corpus. Other effective features indicate that readings as an adjective (9) and as an intransitive verb (20) are not preferred.

Modifiers. Feature 5 indicates the preference to attach prepositional phrases to noun phrases. However, if a modifier is attached to a verb, we prefer readings and realizations where the modifier is left-adjoining rather than right-adjoining (7, 18, 19). For instance, *zij heeft met de hond gelopen* (*she has with the dog walked*) is more fluent than *zij heeft gelopen met de hond* (*she has walked with the dog*). Finally, feature 15 gives preference to analyses where the preposition *van* is a modifier of a noun.

Conjunctions. Two of the twenty most discriminative features involve conjunctions. The first (6) is a dispreference for conjunctions where conjuncts have a varying depth. In conjunctions, the model prefers derivations where all conjuncts in a conjunctions have an equal depth. The other feature (17) gives a preferences to conjunctions with parallel conjuncts — conjunctions where every conjunct is constructed using the same grammar rule.

Punctuation. The Alpino grammar is very generous in allowing optional punctuation. An empty punctuation sign is used to fill grammar rule slots when no punctuation is used or realized. Two features indicate preferences with respect to optional punctuation. The first (10) gives preference to filling the second daughter slot of the *vp_mod_v* with the empty punctuation sign. This implies that derivations are preferred where a modifier and a verb are not separated by punctuation. The second feature (14) indicates a general preference for the occurrence of empty optional punctuation in the derivation tree.

Subjects/objects. In Dutch, subject fronting is preferred over object fronting. For instance, *Spanje won de wereldbeker* (*Spain won the World Cup*) is preferred over *de wereldbeker won Spanje* (*the World Cup won spain*). Feature 8 will in many cases contribute to the preference of having topicalized noun phrase subjects. It disprefers having a noun phrase left of the verb. For example, *zij heeft met de hond gelopen* (*she has with the dog walked*) is preferred over *met de hond heeft zij gelopen* (*with the dog she has walked*). Feature 11 encodes the preference for subject fronting, by penalizing derivations where the topic is a non-subject noun phrase.

Other syntactic preferences. The remaining features are syntactic preferences that do not belong to any of the previous categories. Feature 4 indicates a dispreference for derivations where bare nouns occur. Feature 12 indicates a preference for derivations where a noun occurs along with an adjective. Finally, feature 13 gives preference to the prepositional complement (*pc*) relation if a preposition is a dependent of a verb and lexical analysis shows that the verb can combine with that prepositional complement.

We can conclude from this description of features that many of the features that are paramount to parse disambiguation and fluency ranking are task-independent, modeling phenomena such as subject/object fronting, modifier adjoining, parallelism and depth in conjunctions, and the use of punctuation.

7 Conclusion

In this work we have used feature selection techniques for maximum entropy modeling to analyze the hypothesis that the models in reversible stochastic attribute-value grammars use task-independent features. To this end, we have first compared three feature selection techniques, namely gain-informed selection, grafting, and grafting-light. In this comparison we see that grafting outperforms both grafting-light and gain-informed selection in parse disambiguation and fluency ranking tasks.

We then used grafting to select the most effective features for parse disambiguation, fluency ranking, and reversible models. In the quantitative analysis we have shown that the reversible model does not put more emphasis on task-specific features. In fact, the opposite is true: in the reversible model task-independent features become more defining than in the directional models.

We have also provided a qualitative analysis of the twenty most effective features, showing that many of these features are relevant to both parsing and generation. Effective task-independent features for Dutch model phenomena such as subject/object fronting, modifier adjoining, parallelism and depth in conjunctions, and the use of punctuation.

8 Future work

An approach for testing the reversibility of models that we have not touched upon in this work, is to evaluate such models using tasks that combine parsing and generation. For instance, a good word graph parser should choose a fluent sentence with a syntactically plausible reading. If reversible models integrate parsing-specific, generation-specific, and task-independent features properly, they should be competitive to models specifically trained for that task. In the future, we hope to evaluate reversible stochastic attribute-value grammars in the light of such tasks.

9 Acknowledgments

This work was funded by the DAISY project of the STEVIN program. The author would also like to thank Yan Zhao, Barbara Plank, and Gertjan van Noord for the many valuable discussions on maximum entropy modeling and feature selection.

References

Adam L. Berger, Stephen A. Della Pietra, and Vincent J. Della Pietra. 1996. A maximum entropy approach to natural language processing. *Computational linguistics*, 22(1):71.

Aoife Cahill, Martin Forst, and Christian Rohrer. 2007. Designing features for parse disambiguation and realisation ranking. In *The Proceedings of the LFG '07 Conference*, pages 128–147. CSLI Publications.

Aoife Cahill. 2009. Correlating human and automatic evaluation of a german surface realiser. In *Proceedings of the ACL-IJCNLP 2009 Conference - Short Papers*, pages 97–100.

Daniël de Kok and Gertjan van Noord. 2010. A sentence generator for Dutch. In *Proceedings of the 20th Computational Linguistics in the Netherlands conference (CLIN)*, pages 75–90.

Daniël de Kok, Barbara Plank, and Gertjan van Noord. 2011. Reversible stochastic attribute-value grammars. In *Proceedings of the ACL HLT 2011 Conference - Short Papers*.

Daniël de Kok. 2010. Feature selection for fluency ranking. In *Proceedings of the 6th International Natural Language Generation Conference (INLG)*, pages 155–163.

Mark Johnson and Stefan Riezler. 2000. Exploiting auxiliary distributions in stochastic unification-based grammars. In *Proceedings of the 1st Meeting of the North American Chapter of the Association for Computational Linguistics*, pages 154–161, Seattle, Washington.

Robert Malouf and Gertjan van Noord. 2004. Wide coverage parsing with stochastic attribute value grammars. In *IJCNLP-04 Workshop: Beyond shallow analyses - Formalisms and statistical modeling for deep analyses*. JST CREST, March.

I. Dan Melamed, Ryan Green, and Joseph Turian. 2003. Precision and recall of machine translation. In *HLT-NAACL*.

Miles Osborne. 2000. Estimation of stochastic attribute-value grammars using an informative sample. In *Proceedings of the 18th conference on Computational linguistics (COLING)*, pages 586–592.

Simon Perkins, Kevin Lacker, and James Theiler. 2003. Grafting: Fast, incremental feature selection by gradient descent in function space. *The Journal of Machine Learning Research*, 3:1333–1356.

Stefan Riezler and Alexander Vasserman. 2004. Incremental feature selection and l1 regularization for relaxed maximum-entropy modeling. In *Proceedings of the 2004 Conference on Empirical Methods in Natural Language Processing (EMNLP04), Barcelona, Spain.*

Robert Tibshirani. 1996. Regression shrinkage and selection via the Lasso. *Journal of the Royal Statistical Society. Series B (Methodological)*, pages 267–288.

Leonoor van der Beek, Gosse Bouma, Robert Malouf, and Gertjan van Noord. 2002. The Alpino dependency treebank. In *Computational Linguistics in the Netherlands (CLIN)*.

Gertjan van Noord, Ineke Schuurman, and Gosse Bouma. 2010. Lassy syntactische annotatie, revision 19053. `http://www.let.rug.nl/vannoord/Lassy/sa-man_lassy.pdf`.

Gertjan van Noord. 2006. **At Last Parsing Is Now Operational**. In *TALN 2006 Verbum Ex Machina, Actes De La 13e Conference sur Le Traitement Automatique des Langues naturelles*, pages 20–42, Leuven.

Gertjan van Noord. 2007. Using self-trained bilexical preferences to improve disambiguation accuracy. In *Proceedings of the International Workshop on Parsing Technology (IWPT)*, ACL 2007 Workshop, pages 1–10, Prague. Association for Computational Linguistics, ACL.

Yaqian Zhou, Lide Wu, Fuliang Weng, and Hauke Schmidt. 2003. A fast algorithm for feature selection in conditional maximum entropy modeling. In *Proceedings of the 2003 conference on Empirical methods in natural language processing*, EMNLP '03, pages 153–159, Stroudsburg, PA, USA. Association for Computational Linguistics.

Jun Zhu, Ni Lao, and Eric P. Xing. 2010. Grafting-light: fast, incremental feature selection and structure learning of Markov random fields. In *Proceedings of the 16th ACM SIGKDD international conference on Knowledge discovery and data mining*, pages 303–312. ACM.

Author Index

Association for Computational Linguistics
209 N. Eighth Street
Stroudsburg, Pennsylvania 18360

CURRAN ASSOCIATES INC
proceedings
.com